Top Row: *Mark Twain, F. Scott Fitzgerald, Dorothy Parker*
Center: *George Gershwin, Theodore Roosevelt, Sinclair Lewis*
Bottom: *Willa Cather, George M. Cohan, Enrico Caruso*

At one time, all called New
York

Now, on nearly any
some of the excitement and col
Manhattan's memorable people.

THE STREETS WHERE THEY LIVED

A WALKING GUIDE TO THE RESIDENCES OF FAMOUS NEW YORKERS

Stephen W. Plumb

MarLor Press

THE
STREETS
WHERE THEY
═LIVED═

Grateful acknowledgement for quotations from "Here is New York" and "Good-Bye to Forty-Eighth Street" in Essays of E. B. White, 1977: Harper and Row.

The Streets Where They Lived: *A Walking Guide to the Residences of Famous New Yorkers* is published by MarLor Press, 4304 Brigadoon Dr., St. Paul, Minnesota 55126. Represented to the book trade by Contemporary Books, 180 North Michigan Avenue, Chicago, Illinois 60601

Manufactured in the United States of America

Drawings by **Ruth Caprow**
Cover design by **Georgene Sainati**
Inside design by **Charlie Olson**

Library of Congress Cataloging in Publication Data

Plumb, Stephen W., 1942-
    The streets where they lived.

    "A Marlin Bree book"--T.p. verso.
    Includes indexes.
    1. New York (N.Y.)--Description--1981- --Tours.
1. Celebrities--New York (N.Y.)--Homes and haunts--
Guide-books. 3. Walking--New York (N.Y.)--Guide-books.
4. Dwellings--New York (N.Y.)--Guide-books.
F128.18.P58 1989   917.47'10443   88-92900
ISBN 0-943400-35-X

For my mother

Table of Contents

Introduction

More than any other American city, New York embodies the romance of the past. This is true, in part, because it has been the home over the years of so many notable and celebrated individuals.

A visitor can stand on practically any street in the city and feel engulfed by its colorful history.

Shortly after the Second World War, **E.B. White**, while in a room at the **Algonquin Hotel**, wrote an essay in which he noted that he was at that moment sitting only a few blocks from where **Nathan Hale** was executed, from where **Rudolph Valentino** lay in state, from where **Ernest Hemingway** punched **Max Eastman** in the nose, and from where **Harry Thaw** shot **Stanford White.**

White noted that he was *"probably occupying the very room that any number of exalted and somewise memorable characters sat in..."* New York City, he said, *"carries on its lapel the unexpungeable odor of the long past, so that no matter where you sit...you feel the vibrations of great times and tall deeds, of queer people and events and undertakings."*

This book is a small attempt to capture some of the "vibrations" of that New York past by focusing on many of the famous people who have lived there. Specifically, it is a record of the places in Manhattan where the famous have lived in approximately the past one hundred years. It aims to guide the reader, in a series of short walking tours, street by street, to the actual houses, apartments and hotels where they stayed. It offers, in the form of brief annotations, a thumbnail history of each celebrity's residency at a particular address.

I have selected my group of people from various walks of life. You will find on the following pages individuals who were politicians, artists, musicians, playwrights, poets, actors, comedians, singers, novelists, criminals, journalists, and businessmen. Most of them lived in New York in this century. All were people who were made famous by New York and, in turn, helped to make New York famous.

In presenting this list of New Yorkers, I must emphasize that it is very much a selected one. The more than four hundred people and five hundred addresses in this guide represent one person's choices made from a vast number of possibilities. I have made no attempt to be comprehensive. My aim, instead, has been to give the reader a flavor of the history of a selected number of Manhattan neighborhoods. My personal interests and prejudices are obviously reflected.

New York is a changeless city but it is also changing rapidly. In recent years, hundreds of old residences, especially in midtown Manhattan, have been demolished and replaced, usually by large and often ugly, commercial buildings.

On many blocks, these newer buildings stand very close to older structures of great historic interest. Whenever possible, I have recorded the site of a famous person's former home even when that home no longer stands. Unfortunately, in these cases, your power of imagination is the only window to the past for, with every passing day, another piece of New York's history falls to the bulldozer.

If you have the good fortune to be in New York City, either as a visitor or as a resident, I hope this guide succeeds in helping you discover some of the secrets of the city's past. With it you can walk the streets and find the houses where **Gershwin** and **Berlin** composed their songs, where the **Marx Brothers** played as young boys, where **Scott Fitzgerald** stayed while he waited for **Zelda** to come to New York for their wedding, where **Edna St. Vincent Millay** and **Marianne Moore** wrote many of their poems and **Theodore Dreiser** wrote *Sister Carrie,* where **Babe Ruth** relaxed after hitting a long one at Yankee Stadium.

E.B. White, in another essay, said that over a lifetime, a New Yorker is *"likely to keep on the move, shopping for the perfect arrangement of rooms and vistas, changing his habitation according to fortune, whim, and need. And in every place he abandons he leaves something vital..."*

This book is one small attempt to capture that "something." All of the famous people listed on the following pages have died or moved on. A number of their former residences have disappeared. Yet, on block after block, you can still find, standing as memorials, many of the homes they once inhabited. Their spirits remain present there.

To meet them, all you have to do is start walking.

Manhattan

In Eight Sections

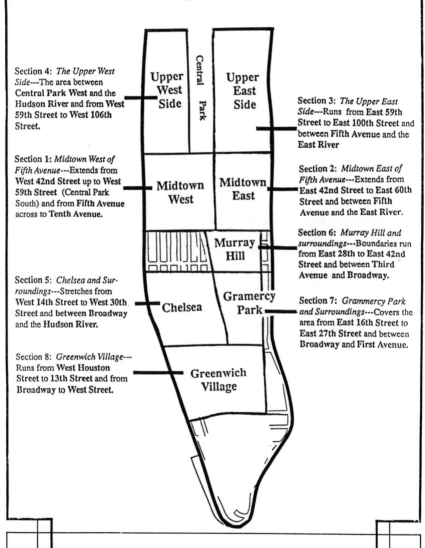

Section 4: *The Upper West Side*---The area between Central Park West and the Hudson River and from West 59th Street to West 106th Street.

Section 1: *Midtown West of Fifth Avenue*---Extends from West 42nd Street up to West 59th Street (Central Park South) and from Fifth Avenue across to Tenth Avenue.

Section 5: *Chelsea and Surroundings*---Stretches from West 14th Street to West 30th Street and between Broadway and the Hudson River.

Section 8: *Greenwich Village*---Runs from West Houston Street to 13th Street and from Broadway to West Street.

Section 3: *The Upper East Side*---Runs from East 59th Street to East 100th Street and between Fifth Avenue and the East River

Section 2: *Midtown East of Fifth Avenue*---Extends from East 42nd Street to East 60th Street and between Fifth Avenue and the East River.

Section 6: *Murray Hill and surroundings*---Boundaries run from East 28th to East 42nd Street and between Third Avenue and Broadway.

Section 7: *Grammercy Park and Surroundings*---Covers the area from East 16th Street to East 27th Street and between Broadway and First Avenue.

Upper West Side

Central Park

Upper East Side

Midtown West

Midtown East

Murray Hill

Chelsea

Gramercy Park

Greenwich Village

About the Guide

This guide is made up of **eight** sections or neighborhoods of Manhattan. Each section is divided into a number of short walking tours, **thirty-six** in all.

Each tour will take anywhere from **fifteen minutes** to an **hour** to cover, depending on the number of places included in that particular tour and the pace that you choose. A **map** is included for each tour.

Each house, apartment, hotel, or other building in the tour is given a **number** corresponding to the same number on the tour **map**. The **text entry** for each building gives the **name** of the person who lived there, the **address**, and a brief **history** of the person's stay, including dates.

The guide is a record of persons either dead or no longer living in New York. Addresses of people currently living in New York are not included in order to protect their privacy.

Index of Persons by Profession

POLITICIANS

Arthur, Chester
Dewey, Thomas E.
Hoover, Herbert
Hughes, Charles Evans
Kennedy, John F.
Kerensky, Alexander
LaGuardia, Fiorello
Lehman, Herbert
Lindsay, John V.
Lodge, Henry Cabot
Moses, Robert
Murphy, Charles
Rockefeller, Nelson
Roosevelt, Franklin D.
Roosevelt, Theodore
Smith, Al
Stevenson, Adlai
Thomas, Norman
Tilden, Samuel
Truman, Harry
Wagner, Robert F.
Wagner, Robert F., Jr.
Walker, Jimmy

MUSICIANS

Arlen, Harold
Bartok, Bela
Beiderbecke, Bix
Berlin, Irving
Bernstein, Leonard
Chaliapin, Feodor
Coltrane, John
Dvorak, Antonin
Dylan, Bob
Ellington, Duke
Gershwin, George
Gershwin, Ira
Gilbert and Sullivan
Goodman, Benny
Hammerstein, Oscar II
Hart, Lorenz
Hendrix, Jimi
Kern, Jerome
Lennon, John
Menuhin, Yehudi
Parker, Charlie
Porter, Cole
Rodgers, Richard
Rubinstein, Artur
Shaw, Artie
Sousa, John Philip

Stokowski, Leopold
Stravinsky, Igor
Thomson, Virgil
Toscanini, Arturo
Weill, Kurt

ARTISTS

Arbus, Diane
Arno, Peter
Bellows, George
Chagall, Marc
Dali, Salvador
DeKooning, Willem
Ernst, Max
Goldberg, Rube
Homer, Winslow
Hopper, Edward
Kertesz, Andre
McMein, Neysa
Manship, Paul
Mondrian, Piet
O'Keeffe, Georgia
Parrish, Maxfield
Pollock, Jackson
Rivers, Larry
Rockwell, Norman
Rothko, Mark
Stieglitz, Alfred

PLAYWRIGHTS

Barry, Philip
Behan, Brendan
Brecht, Bertolt
Chayefsky, Paddy
Connelly, Marc
Coward, Noel
Day, Clarence
Hart, Moss

Hecht, Ben
Hellman, Lillian
Kaufman, George S.
Miller, Arthur
Odets, Clifford
O'Neill, Eugene
Saroyan, William
Sherwood, Robert
Williams, Tennessee

MOVIE PERFORMERS

Astaire, Fred
Bacall, Lauren
Bara, Theda
Bellamy, Ralph
Bergman, Ingrid
Bogart, Humphrey
Bolger, Ray
Brando, Marlon
Brynner, Yul
Burke, Billie
Cagney, James
Carradine, John
Carroll, Madeline
Clair, Rene
Clift, Montgomery
Crawford, Joan
Davies, Marion
Dean, James
Fabray, Nanette
Fairbanks, Douglas
Ferrer, Jose
Fonda, Henry
Gabor, Zsa Zsa
Garbo, Greta
Gardner, Ava
Garfield, John
Gish, Lillian

Goddard, Paulette
Gordon, Ruth
Grable, Betty
Grant, Cary
Hamilton, Margaret
Hayworth, Rita
Hepburn, Katharine
Holliday, Judy
Hudson, Rock
Karloff, Boris
Kelly, Grace
Mankiewicz, Herman
Massey, Raymond
Monroe, Marilyn
O'Brien, Pat
Pickford, Mary
Powell, William
Power, Tyrone
Rathbone, Basil
Russell, Rosalind
Scott, Zachary
Selznick, David
Stanwyck, Barbara
Stewart, Donald Ogden
Stewart, James
Swanson, Gloria
Taylor, Robert
Tierney, Gene
Tone, Franchot
Tracy, Spencer
Valentino, Rudolph
Welles, Orson
West, Mae
Young, Gig

POETS

Auden, W.H.
Benet, Stephen Vincent
Benet, William Rose

Crane, Hart
cummings, e.e.
Lowell, Robert
Masters, Edgar Lee
Millay, Edna St. Vincent
Moore, Clement Clarke
Moore, Marianne
Plath, Sylvia
Robinson, Edwin
  Arlington
Schwartz, Delmore
Teasdale, Sara
Thomas, Dylan
Wylie, Elinor

COMEDIANS

Allen, Fred
Allen, Gracie
Allen, Steve
Benny, Jack
Berle, Milton
Bruce, Lenny
Burns, George
Cox, Wally
Fields, W.C.
Haley, Jack
Hope, Bob
Kaye, Danny
Lahr, Bert
Lewis, Ted
Marx Brothers

WRITERS (PROSE)

Agee, James
Algren, Nelson
Anderson, Sherwood
Bellow, Saul
Barnes, Djuna

Benchley, Robert
Burroughs, William
Cain, James
Caldwell, Erskine
Capote, Truman
Cather, Willa
Cheever, John
Clarke, Arthur C.
Crane, Stephen
Dinesen, Isak
Dos Passos, John
Dreiser, Theodore
Farrell, James T.
Ferber, Edna
Fitzgerald, F. Scott
Hammett, Dashiell
Harte, Bret
Hemingway, Ernest
Henry, O.
Howells, William Dean
Hurst, Fannie
Isherwood, Christopher
James, Henry
Kerouac, Jack
Lardner, Ring
Lewis, Sinclair
Loos, Anita
McCarthy, Mary
McCullers, Carson
Marquand, John
Melville, Herman
Miller, Henry
Nash, Ogden
Nin, Anais
Norris, Frank
O'Hara, John
Parker, Dorothy
Perelman, S.J.
Salinger, J.D.
Steinbeck, John

Thurber, James
Twain, Mark
West, Nathaniel
Wharton, Edith
White, E.B.
Wodehouse, P.G.
Wolfe, Thomas
Wright, Richard

SINGERS

Brice, Fanny
Caruso, Enrico
Clooney, Rosemary
Guthrie, Woody
Holiday, Billie
Jolson, Al
Merman, Ethel
Midler, Bette
Morgan, Helen
Pinza, Ezio
Pons, Lilly
Sinatra, Frank

STAGE PER-
FORMERS

Bankhead, Tallulah
Barrymore, Ethel
Barrymore, John
Bernhardt, Sarah
Booth, Edwin
Booth, Shirley
Cohan, George M.
Cornell, Katharine
Dunnock, Mildred
Fontanne, Lynn
Hayes, Helen
Harrison, Rex
Held, Anna

Lawrence, Gertrude
Lenya, Lotte
Lorraine, Lillian
Lunt, Alfred
McKenna, Siobhan
Mostel, Zero
Page, Geraldine
Robards, Jason
Russell, Lillian
Skinner, Cornelia Otis
Wolheim, Louis
Wooley, Monte

DANCERS

Astaire, Fred and Adele
Balanchine, George
Bolger, Ray
Duncan, Isadora
Lee, Gypsy Rose
Nesbit, Evelyn
Tallchief, Maria
Zorina, Vera

JOURNALISTS

Adams, Franklin P.
Atkinson, Brooks
Broun, Heywood
Cowley, Malcolm
Eastman, Max
Fadiman, Clifton
Grant, Jane
Greeley, Horace
Kilgallen, Dorothy
Lippmann, Walter
Mencken, H.L.
Murrow, Edward R.
Nathan, George Jean
Post, Emily

Reed, John
Rice, Grantland
Runyon, Damon
Ross, Harold
Steffens, Lincoln
Sullivan, Ed
Thompson, Dorothy
Wilson, Edmund
Winchell, Walter
Woollcott, Alexander

**PRODUCERS AND
DIRECTORS
(STAGE AND
SCREEN)**

Belasco, David
Hitchcock, Alfred
Griffith, D.W.
Huston, John
Clurman, Harold
Kaufman, George S.
Kazan, Elia
Logan, Josh
Preminger, Otto
Rose, Billy
Strasberg, Lee
Ziegfeld, Florenz

BUSINESSMEN

Astor, William Waldorf
Baruch, Bernard
Carnegie, Andrew
Duke, James B.
Field, Cyrus
Field, Marshall
Ford, Henry II
Frick, Henry Clay
Getty, J. Paul

Guggenheim, Solomon
Hartford, Huntington
Hearst, William
  Randolph
Hill, James Jerome
Hutton, E.F.
Kennedy, Joseph
Luce, Henry
Morgan, J.P.
Morgan, Pierpont
Nast, Conde
Post, Marjorie
  Merriweather
Pulitzer, Joseph
Pulitzer, Ralph
Rockefeller, John D.
Rockefeller, John D.,Jr.
Ruppert, Jacob
Sarnoff, David
Schwab, Charles M.
Sulzberger, Arthur Hays
Tiffany, Charles
Vanderbilt, Cornelius II
Vanderbilt, Cornelius
Vanderbilt, William H.
Wallace, DeWitt
Whitney, Cornelius
  Vanderbilt
Whitney, John Hay
Whitney, W.C.
Woolworth, Frank W.

CRIMINALS

Anastasia, Albert
Arnstein, Nicky
Becker, Charles
Coll, Vincent
  "Mad Dog"
Costello, Frank

Diamond, Jack "Legs"
Gordon, Waxey
Lansky, Meyer
Luciano, Lucky
Rothstein, Arnold

ATHLETES

Dempsey, Jack
DiMaggio, Joe
Louis, Joe
McGraw, John
Mathewson, Christy
Namath, Joe
Ruth, Babe

MISCELLANEOUS

Adler, Polly
Astor, Mrs. William
Barrymore, Diana
Berkman, Alexander
Bernstein, Aline
Bryant, Louise
Cerf, Bennett
Crater, Judge Joseph
Crosby, Harry
Dodge, Mabel
Duke, Angier Biddle
Eastman, Crystal
Edison, Thomas
Fitzgerald, Zelda
Garroway, Dave
Goldman, Emma
Guggenheim, Peggy
Hammarskjold, Dag
Hand, Learned
Hiss, Alger
Hutton, Barbara
Joyce, Peggy Hopkins

XIII

Section One:

Midtown West of Fifth Avenue

The Plaza Hotel

Immortalized by F. Scott Fitzgerald, it was also home in Manhattan for Frank Lloyd Wright

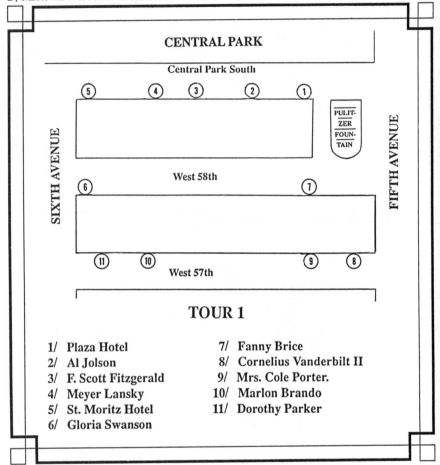

CENTRAL PARK

Central Park South

PULIT-
ZER
FOUN-
TAIN

West 58th

West 57th

TOUR 1

1/ Plaza Hotel
2/ Al Jolson
3/ F. Scott Fitzgerald
4/ Meyer Lansky
5/ St. Moritz Hotel
6/ Gloria Swanson

7/ Fanny Brice
8/ Cornelius Vanderbilt II
9/ Mrs. Cole Porter.
10/ Marlon Brando
11/ Dorothy Parker

Midtown West of Fifth Avenue, extending from **West 42nd Street** up to **West 59th Street** (Central Park South) and from **Fifth Avenue** across to **10th Avenue**, is the part of Manhattan that has probably changed the most in the last 50 years. It can be divided into two basic areas. The **first**, on the streets near **Fifth Avenue** and **Central Park South**, was dominated earlier in this century by large mansions, hotels and brownstones. Although a few of these buildings still stand, the majority were demolished to make way for the modern commercial buildings seen here today. The **second** area, along **Broadway** from **Times Square** to the **West 50's**, was once the heart of New York's entertainment district and filled with great theaters, nightclubs, and restaurants. It was also a residential place with many fine hotels and apartment buildings. Broadway's legitimate theaters still operate here today, though much of the neighborhood has otherwise changed, especially around Times Square. But some wonderful old buildings remain and the streets can be remembered as a place where many celebrated New Yorkers once lived, worked, and played.

Midtown West of Fifth Avenue

Tour 1

1/ Plaza Hotel
Fifth Avenue at 59th Street (Central Park South).

Fitzgerald   Jolson

One of the most beautiful and famous hotels in the world, the **Plaza** has been the host to countless prominent visitors since it opened in 1907. Perhaps its most famous permanent resident was **Frank Lloyd Wright**, whose stays at the Plaza became so frequent over the years that in 1953 he decided to rent Suite 223, overlooking Central Park, on a permanent basis. The front room of his suite was a combination workroom, office, and sitting room where Wright entertained clients, gave interviews, and worked on his designs. His most famous project during his years here was the **Guggenheim Museum** (opened in 1959) whose patron, **Solomon R. Guggenheim**, also had a suite at the hotel. Wright lived here until his death in 1959.

The Plaza played a prominent role in both the real life and in the lives of the fictional characters of novelist **F. Scott Fitzgerald**. The hotel is mentioned in a number of his stories. It is the scene of a party which plays an important part of his novel, *The Great Gatsby*. Fitzgerald and his wife, **Zelda**, came from St. Paul to New York in March, 1922, to celebrate the publication of his second novel, *The Beautiful and Damned,* and lived here at the Plaza for a month. Their stay turned out to be a continual round of parties with both of them drunk most of the time. In September, 1922, they moved back to New York from Minnesota and lived in a suite here while they looked for a house. It was at the Plaza that Fitzgerald met fellow novelist, **John Dos Pasos**. Earlier in his career, when his first novel was being published, Fitzgerald, seeing the Plaza "all blazing with green and gold lights, and the taxis and limousines streaming up and down Fifth Avenue, jumped in the **Pulitzer Fountain** just out of sheer joy." The fountain is located in the plaza east of the hotel and facing Fifth Avenue.

2/ Al Jolson
36 W. 59th St. (Central Park South) between 5th and 6th Avenue.

The building next to the Plaza is the modern **Park Lane Hotel**, built in 1971. But in the 1920's, brownstone apartment buildings stood on this spot and **Al Jolson**, probably at the height of his popularity, moved here in 1922 with his second wife, **Alma Osborne**. He was starring in the hit musical revue *Bombo* playing down the street at the **Jolson 59th Street Theater** on 7th Avenue. In the 1960's, **Ethel Merman** lived here at the Park Lane Hotel.

3/ F. Scott and Zelda Fitzgerald
38 W. 59th St. (Central Park South) between Fifth and Sixth Avenue.

In the fall of 1920, newlyweds Scott and Zelda rented an apartment here, on the present site of the **Park Lane Hotel**. They had their meals sent in from the Plaza Hotel next door. Scott alternated parties and heavy drinking with work on his second novel, *The Beautiful and Damned*. In 1921, the Fitzgeralds left New York for their first trip to Europe.

4/ Meyer Lansky
40 Central Park S. between Fifth and Sixth Avenue.

In 1948, **Lansky** was one of the most powerful bosses of organized crime when he moved into a penthouse here soon after his marriage to his second wife, **Teddie**. He lived here for six years. In 1953, after being released from prison where he had served a short sentence for gambling activities, he left New York permanently, moving to Florida where he felt safer from the probes of federal authorities. It was in that year that he took control of the gambling casinos of Havana in partnership with Cuban dictator **Fulgencio Batista**.

Swanson

5 / St. Moritz Hotel
50 Central Park S. at Sixth Avenue.

This was mainly an apartment hotel when it opened in 1931, and for years it advertised itself as the "biggest little hotel in town." Columnist **Walter Winchell** had an apartment here for many years. He threatened to move out in the early 1930's when the hotel offered gangster **Lucky Luciano** an apartment. Luciano went to the Waldorf-Astoria instead. Winchell supposedly lived at the St. Moritz rent-free for mentioning the hotel's name in his *Daily Mirror* column from time to time. Composer **Kurt Weill** and **Lotte Lenya**, escaping Nazi Germany, made this their first home in America, living here in 1935. In 1941, artist **Marc Chagall**, fleeing the Nazi occupation of Paris, stayed here with his wife, **Bella**.

6 / Gloria Swanson
68 W. 58th St. at Sixth Avenue.

The actress moved into a penthouse on the top floor of this building, then called the **Park Chambers Hotel**, in 1925. It was a few months after her marriage to her third husband, **Henri de la Falaise**. They were divorced in 1931. Swanson split her time between New York and Hollywood and lived in this building until the early 1930's.

7 / Fanny Brice
8 W. 58th St. near Fifth Avenue.

On this site across from the back of the **Plaza Hotel** (where the **Solo Building** now stands), the singer and comedienne rented a duplex apartment in 1914. She was starring in the Ziegfeld Follies at the time. Brice lived here with gambler **Nicky Arnstein** until 1918. In that year Arnstein divorced his first wife and married Fanny.

8 / Cornelius Vanderbilt II
1 W. 57th St. at Fifth Avenue.

The Bergdorf Goodman store stands here now but from 1883 until 1927 this entire corner of Fifth Avenue from 57th to 58th Street was dominated by Vanderbilt's mammoth Victorian mansion. It had 137 rooms. Across the street where the Crown Building now stands, at 2 W. 57th St., stood the house of financier and politician **W.C. Whitney**. Next door at 6 W. 57th was one of the early homes of Theodore Roosevelt who moved there with his family in 1874 at the age of sixteen. (See Section Seven, Tour 2, Number 1 for his first home.)

9 / Mrs. Cole Porter
17 W. 57th St. near Fifth Avenue.

Cole Porter's wife for 35 years was Linda Lee Thomas, a well-born socialite and divorcee whom he met in 1918. When she stayed in New York during the period of their courtship, she lived in a townhouse on this site (now occupied by the huge and ugly **Solow Building**). She also maintained a residence in France. Cole and Linda were married in Paris in December, 1919. When they returned to New York in the early 20's, they lived in an apartment on Fifth Avenue. (See Section Two, Tour 1, No. 21.)

10 / Marlon Brando
53 W. 57th St. between Fifth and Sixth Avenue.

In 1949, **Brando** and his close friend, actor and comedian **Wally Cox**, took a two-room apartment in a building on this site. Brando had recently achieved stardom for his role in *A Streetcar Named Desire*. They lived a rather bohemian existence together, with Cox pursuing his interests in silversmithing, model trains, and playing his recorder while Brando delved into Zen Buddhism, bongo playing, yoga, and fencing. They made their way around Manhattan on motorcycles. The apartment was a Grand Central Station for aspiring actors, assorted intellectuals, and local characters. While he lived here, Brando went to Hollywood, where he made his first three movies, *The Men*, *A Streetcar Named Desire*, and *Viva Zapata*. Cox and Brando split up housekeeping in 1951 when Cox became impatient with Brando's pet raccoon -- the animal enjoyed eating Cox's suits and shoes.

11/ Dorothy Parker, Neysa McMein
57 W. 57th St. between Fifth and Sixth Avenue.

Parker had a cheaply furnished apartment in a three-story red brick building on this site in the early 1920's when she wrote for Vanity Fair and later while she worked as a free-lancer. She moved here with her first husband, **Edwin Parker**, in 1920 and lived alone after they separated. It was a tiny place but she was hardly ever there, except to sleep. She said that all she needed was enough space to "lay a hat--and a few friends." The only things that belonged to her there were a portable typewriter, a dog named Woodrow Wilson, and a canary she named Onan because he spilled his seed on the ground.

Across the hall from Parker was the studio of magazine illustrator **Neysa McMein** who lived here from 1920 to 1926. McMein was a member of the **Algonquin Round Table** and her studio

Parker   **Rockefeller**

functioned as New York's most fashionable salon of the 1920's, often hosting the city's most famous artists, writers, actors and entertainers. A charming and free-spirited woman, McMein attracted the likes of **Charlie Chaplin**, **Harpo Marx**, and **George Gershwin**, all of whom came to her place here to entertain and be entertained.

Tour 2

1/ Nelson Rockefeller
22 W. 55th St. between Fifth and Sixth Avenue.

As governor of New York from 1958 to 1973, **Rockefeller** ran the affairs of the state not from the capitol in Albany, but from his offices in this building. (The building is no longer numbered 22; it is now No. 20.) These offices were connected to a townhouse, back-to-back, at 13 W. 54th St., which was also owned by Rockefeller (see Number 5 below). The building, recently renovated, is now the offices of **Privatbanken**.

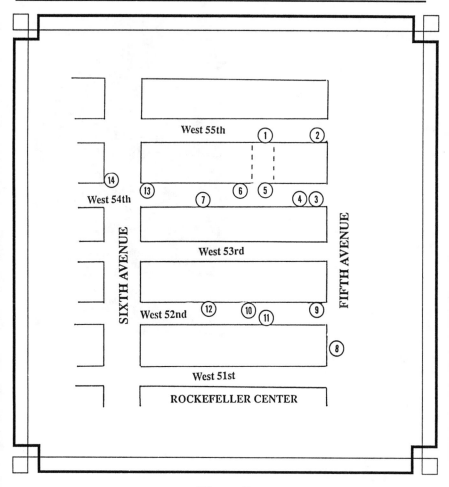

Tour 2

1/ Nelson Rockefeller
2/ Hotel Gotham
3/ John D. Rockefeller, Sr.
4/ John D. Rockefeller, Jr.
5/ Nelson Rockefeller.
6/ Gertrude Lawrence
7/ Eddie Rickenbacker

8/ William H. Vanderbilt
9/ Charlie Parker
10/ Twenty-one Club
11/ Mark Rothko
12/ Marlon Brando
13/ Hotel Warwick
14/ Ziegfeld Theater

2/ Hotel Gotham
2 W. 55th St. at Fifth Avenue.

This ornate, Beaux Arts hotel, which opened in 1906 and was renovated in 1981, was fashionable over the years with stage and movie people. **Damon Runyon** lived here in the 1920's. **Tallulah Bankhead** was a permanent resident in the 1940's as was **Franchot Tone**. **Alexander Woollcott** was living here in 1943 when he died. The hotel reopened in 1988 under new ownership and is now **Hotel Maxim's**.

3/ John D. Rockefeller, Sr.
4 W. 54th St. between Fifth and Sixth Avenue.

The founder of **Standard Oil Company** moved into a four-story brownstone mansion on this site with his family in 1884. The house, built in 1865, was purchased for $600,000. At the time he moved in, it had large lawns on both sides. Rockefeller loved ice-skating and replaced the lawns with rinks in the wintertime. Many mornings, before and after the work day, spectators could see him skating there. The house was demolished in 1936. Rockefeller died in 1937.

4/ John D. Rockefeller, Jr.
10 W. 54th St. between Fifth and Sixth Avenue.

Rockefeller's oldest son, the world-famous philanthropist, moved into a large house on this site in 1908 with his wife, **Abby Green Aldrich**. It was next door to his father's house. They lived here until 1936.

John D. Rockefeller Senior and Junior

It was here that they raised their six children: daughter, **Abigail,** and five sons, **John 3rd**, **Nelson**, **Laurance**, **Winthrop**, and **David**.

5/ John D. Rockefeller, Jr. and Nelson Rockefeller
13 W. 54th St. between Fifth and Sixth Avenue.

Rockefeller, Jr. moved to this house in 1901 soon after his marriage. He lived here until 1908 when his son, **Nelson**, was born. At that time they moved to a house across the street at 10 W. 54th St. (see Number 4 above). Nelson owned the house here at 13 W. 54th St. in later years and it was here that he died suddenly of a heart attack on

Rickenbacker

December 26, 1979. He was 71 years old.

6/ Gertrude Lawrence
17 W. 54th St. between Fifth and Sixth Avenue.

The actress and comedienne moved into this attractive building called the **Rockefeller Apartments** when it first opened in 1936. Her apartment looked out on the garden of the **Museum of Modern Art.**

Lawrence gave some of her most memorable stage performances during her years here. She played the role of the governess in the original production of *The King and I,* which opened in

1951. She died while she was living here in September, 1952, at age 52.

7/ Eddie Rickenbacker
30 W. 54th St. between Fifth and Sixth Avenue.

The World War I flying ace lived here at the **Dorset Hotel** during the last years of his life. He died in 1973.

New Yorker cartoonist **Peter Arno** also made the Dorset his home.

8/ William H. Vanderbilt
Fifth Avenue between 51st and 52nd Street (west side).

William H. Vanderbilt was the son of railroad tycoon **Cornelius Vanderbilt.** He built two massive Victorian brownstone mansions on this block in 1888, one for himself, one for his daughter. They were demolished in 1927 and 1947.

Vanderbilt

West 52nd between **Fifth** and **Sixth** Avenue is today a typical commercial street in midtown Manhattan, with modern office buildings and stores lining its entire length. There is little trace of what it was 40 years ago when it was simply known as **the Street**---the place to go in New York to hear the best jazz, the best comedians, the best singers.

Early in this century, **West 52nd Street** was an upper middle class neighborhood filled with five-story brownstones, but by the 1920's and Prohibition, many of the street -level interiors were turned into speakeasies, and, after Repeal they became nightclubs and restaurants. By the war years there were more bars and bistros here than anywhere else in the city. It was these clubs, places with names like the **Famous Door**, the **Onyx**, the **Downbeat**, and the **Three Deuces**, that spawned such jazz greats as **Art Tatum, Billie Holliday, Coleman Hawkins, Fats Waller, Erroll Garner, Teddy Wilson**, and **Sara Vaughan**. It was here that a new kind of jazz was developed called *"bebop,"* a style most often associated with the name of saxophonist **Charlie Parker**, who spent a lot of time on this street playing in its clubs and living here as well.

It was also in nightclubs like **Leon and Eddie's** that many notable comedians, including **Milton Berle, Jackie Gleason, Jerry Lewis**, and **Jackie Leonard**, got a hearing---often their first. By the early 1950's, a number of factors including high rents, drugs, prostitution, and organized crime led to the demise of West 52nd Street. Strip-tease clubs and clip-joints blossomed and the good music fled elsewhere. One by one the old buildings were demolished and replaced by the modern towers found here today. West 52nd Street has since been designated as **"Swing Street"** to commemorate its unique place in jazz history.

9/ Charlie (Bird) Parker
7 W. 52nd St. at Fifth Avenue.

On the site where the **Tishman Building** now stands was an old, three-story brownstone house frequented by the many jazz musicians who lived in this block in the late 1940's. It was the home of a young woman named **Chan Richardson** who made it into a 24-hour crash pad where the musicians were always welcome.

Charlie Parker became a frequent visitor to the "open house" at 7 W. 52nd St. in 1944-45. During this time he formed the first small bebop band with **Dizzy Gillespie** at the **Three Deuces**, a club across the street from Richardson's house. Parker and Richardson became

friends, then lovers, and he lived in the house for a period in the late 40's. This corner of the block was demolished in 1957 when the Tishman Building replaced it. Across the street at 6 W. 52nd St., the Wall Street millionaire **Bernard Baruch** lived in a four-story brownstone from 1905 until the early 1920's.

10/ Twenty-one Club
21 W. 52nd St. between Fifth and Sixth Avenue.

This famous club, once known as **Jack and Charlie's**, opened as a speakeasy in 1930. It soon became a celebrity haunt, attracting the **Algon-**

quin **Roundtable** crowd and their likes. During Prohibition, its success depended on ingenuity as much as anything else: elaborate gadgets including a trapdoor on the bar that tipped alcoholic drinks into the sewer at the press of a button and cellars with a secret door were safeguards against police raids.

After 1933, Twenty-one became a legitimate restaurant and it is still very popular today, drawing the same kinds of celebrities that brought it its reputation. On West 52nd Street, it is the only reminder left of that era before and after the Second World War.

11/ Mark Rothko
22 W. 52nd St. between Fifth and Sixth Avenue.

In 1945, the artist moved into a brownstone apartment on this site where Warner Communications now stands (part of Rockefeller Plaza). **Rothko** and wife, **Mel**, made this part of midtown Manhattan home for the next 15 years, living in apartments or studios that have now all been replaced by modern buildings.

In late 1946, Rothko and Mell moved around the corner from here to 1288 Sixth Ave. at 52nd Street where the huge **Sperry Building** now stands. They lived there until 1954 when they moved two blocks north to 102 W. 54th St., where the **Hilton Hotel** now stands. In 1960 they moved to the Upper East Side.

12/ Marlon Brando
37 W. 52nd St. between Fifth and Sixth Avenue.

In 1948 a famous nightclub and restaurant called **Leon and Eddie's** stood on the site of this glass office building. **Brando,** who was appearing on Broadway in the role of Stanley Kowalski in *A Streetcar Named Desire*, stayed in an old brownstone next door. He lived his real life much like Kowalski. The room, with a communal bath down the hall, had mattresses on the floor, no chairs, a hi-fi set, bongo drums, and barbells. Brando traveled around town with his friend, **Wally Cox,** on a motorcycle.

13/ Hotel Warwick
65 W. 54th St. at Sixth Avenue (northeast corner).

This attractive hotel was originally built for residential occupancy by **William Randolph Hearst** in the 1920's during the period when he was rapidly expanding his real estate empire. Singer-actress **Helen Morgan** lived here with her mother, **Lulu,** beginning in 1927 when she starred in the musical, *Show Boat,* which played across the street at the **Ziegfeld Theater**. (Her famous nightclub, which was opened in 1928 and later closed by prohibition agents, was at 134 W. 52nd St. on a spot where office buildings now stand.)

Actor **John Garfield** lived in a suite at the Warwick in 1952 after separating from his wife.

14/ Ziegfeld Theatre
1341 Sixth Ave. at West 54th St. (northwest corner).

Directly across the street from the Warwick Hotel, where the **Burlington House** now stands, is the site where **William Randolph Hearst** built the famous **Ziegfeld Theater** in 1927. It was designed by Joseph Urban.

The home of the **Ziegfeld Follies** from 1913 until 1927 had been the **New Amsterdam Theater** (which still stands empty at Broadway and 42nd Street). Ziegfeld opened his new theater here with **Jerome Kern's** hit musical Show Boat, starring **Helen Morgan**. The last Follies played here in 1931

After Ziegfeld's death in 1932, **Billy Rose** purchased the theater and restored it. The building was demolished in 1967.

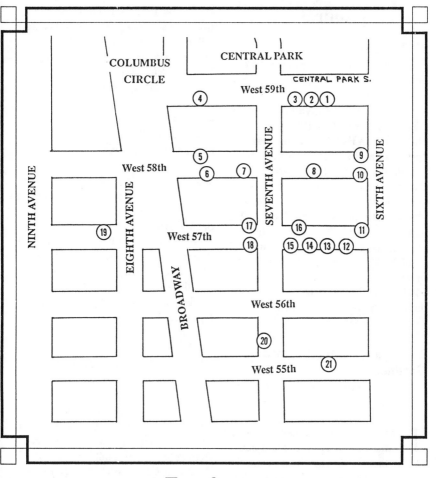

Tour 3

1/ Ritz-Carlton
2/ Hampshire House
3/ Essex House
4/ Artie Shaw
5/ Harold Ross
6/ Judy Holliday
7/ George S. Kaufman
8/ Marlon Brando
9/ Anais Nin
10/ Fred Allen
11/ Damon Runyon

12/ Isadora Duncan
13/ William Dean Howells
14/ Marc Connelly
15/ Carnegie Hall Studios
16/ Anita Loos
17/ The Osborne Apartments
18/ Theodore Dreiser
19/ Bela Bartok
20/ Park Central Hotel
21/ Tennessee Williams

Tour 3

1/ Ritz-Carlton
112 Central Park S. between Sixth and Seventh Avenue.

This newly renovated building which opened in 1982 is the new **Ritz-Carlton Hotel.** It was formerly the **Navarro,** a prominent apartment hotel for many years. Prizefighter **Jack Dempsey** lived here with his third wife, **Hannah,** in 1934 and 1935. **Random House** publisher **Bennett Cerf** had a four-room apartment here in the late 1930's, as a bachelor, and remained until 1941 when he married. The original Ritz-Carlton Hotel stood at Madison and 46th Street until it was demolished in 1951 (see Section Two, Tour 4, Number 11).

2/ Frank Sinatra and Ava Gardner
150 Central Park S. between Sixth and Seventh Avenue.

The pair made this elegant apartment complex called the **Hampshire House** their New York home from the beginning of their courtship in 1948 until their marriage in 1951. **Ingrid Bergman** lived here in 1946 while she played the role of *Joan of Arc* on Broadway.

3/ Essex House
160 Central Park S. between Sixth and Seventh Avenue.

Built in 1930, **Essex House** has been a favorite residence of show business people over the years. **Milton Berle** and **Betty Grable** lived here in the 1940's. **George Burns** and **Gracie Allen** were living here in 1934 when they adopted their first child. Composer **Igor Stravinsky** lived here from 1969 until his death in 1971.

4/ Artie Shaw
222 Central Park S. between Seventh Avenue and Broadway.

In the early 1940's, the bandleader lived here at the **Gainsborough,** a famous studio apartment building opened in 1907 for artists and would-be artists. Shaw, who had wed and divorced starlet **Lana Turner** in 1940, (they were married just seven months) was then at the height of his popularity and led one of the most prominent of the big bands.

5 / Harold Ross
231 W. 58th St. between Seventh Avenue and Broadway.

The editor of the *New Yorker* lived in a small walk-up apartment on this site with his first wife, **Jane Grant,** from August, 1920, until August, 1922. Ross and Grant were struggling journalists at that time, working for other people's publications. It wasn't until February 21, 1925, that the first issue of the *New Yorker* appeared on the newsstands.

6/ Judy Holliday
226 W. 58th St. between Seventh Avenue and Broadway.

As an 18-year old actress in 1940-41, she shared an apartment here with a woman friend. The building was a newly renovated brownstone then, and their rooms were brightly lit by twin skylights. The rent was $57 a month.

7/ George S. Kaufman
200 W. 58th St. between Seventh Avenue and Broadway.

As a young playwright, **Kaufman** and his wife, **Beatrice**, had an apartment in this building from 1921 until 1929. During that time he collaborated on such plays as *Merton of the Movies* with **Marc Connelly**, and *The Cocoanuts* and *Animal Crackers* with **Morrie Ryskind**, both of which starred the **Marx Brothers**.

8/ Marlon Brando
158 W. 58th St. between Sixth and Seventh Avenue.

In 1944, as a 21-year-old Broadway actor, and still living a bohemian existence, Brando lived here at the **Park Savoy** with a girlfriend named **Celia Webb**. It was during this period that he appeared in the play, *Truckline Cafe* which brought him his first rave notices.

9 / Anais Nin
101 W. 58th St. at Sixth Avenue (northwest corner).

Now the renovated **Trump Parc** apartments, this building, across from the **Helmsley Windsor Hotel**, was the **Barbizon-Plaza Hotel** and it was here that Nin lived from November 1934 until the spring of 1935. She called the place the "Hotel Chaotica."

Nin had just returned to New York from Paris and spent the months here studying psychoanalysis with her mentor, **Otto Rank**. Writer **Henry Miller**, still in love with her and jealous of her involvement with Rank, followed her from Paris and stayed with her at the hotel in February 1935. Nin returned to France in May of that year.

Mob leader **Lucky Luciano** also lived in this hotel in the late 1920's.

10/ Fred Allen
100 W. 58th St. at Sixth Avenue (southwest corner).

The **Windsor Hotel** (now called the **Helmsley Windsor**) was the New York home of radio comedian Allen in the 1930's and 40's. He lived here with his wife, **Portland**.

11/ Damon Runyon
101 W. 57th St. at Sixth Avenue (northwest corner).

The creator of *Guys and Dolls* lived at this residential hotel, called the **Buckingham,** from 1944 until the end of his life. He moved here after separating from his last wife. It was in that year that cancer was discovered in his throat; as a result of the surgery, he lost his voice permanently.

At the Buckingham, if he needed service, he would raise the telephone and tinkle a small bell---a signal to the desk clerk to dispatch a bell boy to his rooms. Runyon died December 10, 1946.

12/ Isadora Duncan, William Saroyan
118 W. 57th St. between Sixth and Seventh Avenue.

Now the luxurious Parker Meridien, this building was for many years the **Great Northern Hotel**. Dancer **Isadora Duncan**, then 45 years old, lived here in 1922-23 with her new husband, Russian poet, **Sergei Esenin**. While here, she made a controversial U.S. dance tour which brought her into frequent conflict with local authorities because of her daring stage costumes and her outspoken political comments. Duncan gave her final American performances in January, 1923, at **Carnegie Hall** (a few doors up from their hotel) and then left the country for the last time. She died in France in 1927.

William Saroyan, soon after gaining his first success as a short story writer, lived at the Great Northern in 1935, before traveling to Europe. By then the hotel was becoming run-down. In his room here, he wrote his first play after reading in the *New York Times* the mistaken report that he was at work on a drama.

13 / William Dean Howells
120 W. 57th St. between Sixth and Seventh Avenue.

The novelist who wrote *The Rise of Silas Lapham* lived in an apartment in this building, then called the **Hotel St. Hubert,** for the last ten years of his life. He died here in his sleep on May 11, 1920, at the age of 84.

14/ Marc Connelly
152 W. 57th St. between Sixth and Seventh Avenue.

The playwright who won the **Pulitzer Prize** in 1930 for *Green Pastures* lived in an apartment building called the **Rembrandt** on this site from the mid-1920's until 1935. Located between the **Russian Tea Room** and **Carnegie Hall**, the Rembrandt was built in 1881 and, now demolished, was reputedly New York's first duplex apartment house. In 1929, Connelly was a bachelor living with his mother here when he began to write his famous play. He moved to 25 Central Park W. in 1935 and lived there until his death in 1980.

15 / Carnegie Hall Studios
160 W. 57th St. at Seventh Avenue.

Carnegie Hall, opened in 1891, is most famous for its concert auditorium. Less well known is the fact that it contains offices, studios, apartments, and stores. The 15-story tower above the auditorium has approximately 170 studios which were originally built to provide working and living spaces for artists and musicians. Among the many who have lived here over the years are **John Barrymore, Marc Connelly, Paddy Chayefsky, Marlon Brando** and **John Philip Sousa.**

16/ Anita Loos
171 W. 57th St. at Seventh Avenue.

The Hollywood screenwriter, playwright, and novelist lived in an apartment in this building during the

The Osborne
Former home of Gig Young, Ethel Barrymore, Leonard Bernstein

last decade of her life. Loos was probably best known as the author of the satirical novel, *Gentlemen Prefer Blonds,* written in 1925 and later made into a movie with **Marilyn Monroe**. Loos died while living here in 1981 at age 93.

17/ The Osborne
205 W. 57th St. at Seventh Avenue (northwest corner).

This large red-stone building, erected in 1885, has been the home of many famous New Yorkers. **Leonard Bernstein** wrote the score for *West Side Story* while he lived here. Other residents were **Ralph Bellamy, Shirley Booth, Virgil Thomson, Harold Clurman, Ethel Barrymore**, and **Gig Young**.

18/ Theodore Dreiser
200 W. 57th St. at Seventh Avenue (southwest corner).

The novelist lived here at the **Rodin Studios** from late 1927 until 1931. He moved into a duplex apartment on the 13th and 14th floor for $3,500 a year---rent he could finally afford due to the great success of his novel, *An American Tragedy.* His long-time companion, **Helen Patges Richardson**, stayed with him. The Rodin Studios have now been converted into offices.

19/ Bela Bartok
309 W. 57th St. between Eighth and Ninth Avenue.

The Hungarian composer lived in this building during the last year of his life. He died in 1945. A plaque on the wall commemorates his passing.

20/ Park Central Hotel
870 Seventh Ave. between 55th and 56th Street.

This famous hotel, now called the **Omni Park Central**, was the home of the widowed **Eleanor Roosevelt** from 1949 until 1953, and then again in 1958. It was known as the **Park Sheraton** in those days.

Columnist **Walter Winchell** lived here with his wife and family in the early 1930's. The great movie director, **D.W. Griffith**, then in sad decline, lived here in 1933. Boxer **Joe Louis** lived here in the 1960's.

Park Central was also the scene of two of the most sensational underworld murders in New York history. On November 4, 1928, gambler **Arnold Rothstein**, then known as the *"J.P. Morgan of the underworld,"* its banker and master of strategy, was shot in Room 349, allegedly because he had failed to pay a gambling debt. He died two days later. On October 25, 1957, Brooklyn mob boss **Albert Anastasia** was shot to death by unidentified assailants while he sat in the barber shop just inside the front entrance on Seventh Avenue. Both murders remain unsolved.

21/ Tennessee Williams
145 W. 55th St. between Sixth and Seventh Avenue.

In 1965-66, the playwright subleased a penthouse in this 15-story building next to the **City Center Theater**. In mourning over the death of his lover,

Frank Merlo, Williams became a virtual recluse at that time. "When he died," Williams wrote, "I went to pieces. I retreated into a shell. I wouldn't speak to a living soul." He fell into a world of drink, drugs, and depression that lasted until the end of the decade. Ironically he was at the peak of his fame and financial success during this same period.

Tour 4

1 / Algonquin Hotel
59 W. 44th St. between Fifth and Sixth Avenue

The **Algonquin** has retained its status as a literary landmark over the years. In the early 1920's, its **Rose Room** was the meeting place for America's most famous luncheon club, the **Round Table**. Regulars included **Dorothy Parker**, **George S. Kaufman**, **Harold Ross**, **Robert Sherwood**, **Alexander Woollcott**, **Robert Benchley**, **Edna Ferber**, **Ring Lardner**, and **Franklin P. Adams**.

The Algonquin opened in 1902 and its literary reputation emerged in 1914 when **H.L. Mencken** stayed here during the period when he began to co-edit the magazine *The Smart Set* with **George Jean Nathan**, who lived at the **Royalton Hotel** across the street.

James Thurber made this his home for long periods in the 1930's and also in the 1950's when he visited New York from his home in Connecticut. He was staying here on the night of October 4, 1961 when he suffered the stroke that took his life a month later. **F. Scott Fitzgerald** lived here for a period in 1934 while he waited for the publication

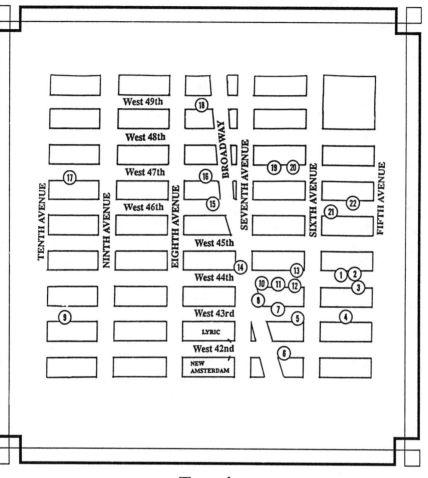

Tour 4

1/ Algonquin Hotel
2/ James Dean
3/ Royalton Hotel
4/ George Gershwin
5/ Woody Guthrie
6/ Hotel Knickerbocker
7/ Metropole Hotel
8/ Eugene O'Neill
9/ Tennessee Williams
10/ Lucky Luciano
11/ The Lambs Club

12/ Bix Beiderbecke
13/ David Belasco
14/ Hotel Astor
15/ Cary Grant
16/ Hotel Edison
17/ Harold Ross
18/ Hotel Forrest
19/ Lenny Bruce
20/ Coolidge Hotel
21/ Delmore Schwartz
22/ Irving Berlin

of his novel, *Tender is the Night.* Silent-screen star **Douglas Fairbanks** lived here from 1907 to 1915; he did his macho gymnastics on the roof of the hotel. The Algonquin continues to be a popular stopping-place for literary and theater people today.

2/ James Dean
49 W. 44th St. between Fifth and Sixth Avenue.

The legendary film star lived in Room 802 of the **Iroquois Hotel** with a friend in 1951. He was a struggling 20-year-old actor at the time. They couldn't afford the more expensive **Algonquin** next door---so they paid $90 a month to live here. Friends say he had a small model of a gallows in the apartment, specially lit from behind so that it projected the huge shadow of a noose; it was the first thing a visitor saw on entering Dean's apartment.

3/ Royalton Hotel
44 W. 44th St. between Fifth and Sixth Avenue.

This hotel is probably best known as the longtime home of **George Jean Nathan.** Nathan, who, along with **H.L. Mencken,** co-edited the famous literary magazine, *The Smart Set,* from 1914-1925, had an apartment here from 1908 until his death in 1959. Humorist **Robert Benchley** lived here off and on over the years. **William Saroyan** stayed at the Royalton on his long visits to New York in the last years of his life. He was staying here in the early 40's when he won the **Pulitzer Prize** for *The Time of Your Life.* (The original offices of both *The Smart Set* and the *New Yorker* are just a block away, in a building at 25 W. 45th St. The *New Yorker* started there in 1925; *The Smart Set* operated there from 1914 to 1923.)

4/ George Gershwin
34 W. 43rd St. between Fifth and Sixth Avenue.

This building was erected in 1912 and redesigned in 1970 as the **Graduate Center of the City University of New York.** On the third floor was an old auditorium called the **Aeolian Hall** and here, on February 12, 1924, Gershwin performed his *Rhapsody in Blue* for the first time. **Paul Whiteman** was the conductor.

5/ Woody Guthrie
West 43rd Street and Sixth Avenue (southwest corner).

The legendary folksinger was 27 in 1940 when he arrived in New York for the first time. In February he took a room in this storefront building, then a fleabag hotel called the **Hanover House.** It was here that he wrote the song, *"This Land is Your Land,"* as an angry response to **Irving Berlin's** *"God Bless America."*

6/ Hotel Knickerbocker
142 W. 42nd St. at Broadway (southeast corner).

Offices now fill this classical, brick-and-limestone building with the mansard roof. But for years it was one of New York's most famous hotels. The

Caruso

friends. On the day he left the hotel, he forgot to turn off the faucets in the bathtub and the room was flooded.

New Amsterdam Theater and Lyric Theater
Broadway at West 42nd Street.

As we walk up Broadway at 42nd Street, we pass two landmarks of American theatrical history:

The **New Amsterdam Theater** (214 W. 42nd St., near the southwest corner of Broadway) was built in 1903 and was the premier musical comedy theater in New York. It was the home of the **Ziegfeld Follies** from 1913 until 1927, when **Ziegfeld** built his own theater. Broadway's greatest stars played here. **Fred and Adele Astaire** and **Ruby Keeler** performed on a stage considered the best ever built for dancing. The rooftop included another theater with glass balconies, rainbow lighting, a movable stage, and a famous nightclub called the **Midnight Frolic.** The New Amsterdam became a Kung Fu movie house before it closed in 1983. A plan by government and community organizations to build a playhouse for regional theater productions in the roof garden has been stalled in recent years. Renovation is still pending.

Knickerbocker was commissioned by **John Jacob Astor** and opened in 1902. Probably its most famous resident was **Enrico Caruso**, who lived in a 14-room apartment here on the ninth floor from 1908 until 1920. On the day of the false Armistice in 1918, from a corner balcony, he sang the *"Star Spangled Banner"* to a crowd in Times Square. He moved away in 1920 when the hotel was sold---a transaction which he regarded as a personal affront.

George M. Cohan lived here at one time. Silent-screen actress **Mary Pickford** was living here in 1916 when she met actor **Douglas Fairbanks** whom she later married.

In 1920, flushed with the excitement of having his first novel published, **F.Scott Fitzgerald** stayed here briefly, boozing and lavishly entertaining his

Across the street at 213 W. 42nd St. stands the **Lyric Theatre**.

Also opened in 1903, it was the scene of many hit plays and musical comedies with stars like **Fairbanks, Jolson**, and the **Astaires**. One of the memorable shows of the twenties played at the Lyric---it was the **Marx Brothers** starring in **George S. Kaufman's** *The Cocoanuts,* which opened on December 8, 1925, with music by **Irving Berlin**. The play was later turned into the Marx Brothers' first movie of the same name. The Lyric became a movie theater in 1933. It continues to be one today, although the setting of this street has sadly changed, much for the worse.

7/ Metropole Hotel

149 West 43rd Street east of Broadway (near the northeast corner).

At the turn of the century on this site, where modern office buildings now stand, was the **Metropole Hotel**. Here on July 16, 1912, on the sidewalk in front of the entrance, gambler **Herman Rosenthal** was shot down by four mobsters. The shooting led to one of the most sensational criminal trials in New York history, involving police corruption at the highest levels, and when it was over, five men including police lieutenant **Charles Becker** were executed in the Sing Sing electric chair. The murder scene is described in **Fitzgerald's** *The Great Gatsby.*

8/ Eugene O'Neill

West 43rd Street at Broadway (northeast corner).

The playwright was born on this site, later to be the heart of the theater district, in a family style hotel called the **Barrett House**, on October 16, 1888. At that time, his father, actor **James O'Neill** had begun his sixth season in the role that made him famous, *The Count of Monte Cristo.* Known today for its vice and urban decay, there is no trace on this corner of the atmosphere of that time. The area was called **Longacre Square**. Sixteen years later, it was renamed **Times Square**. Behind the Barrett House were comfortable houses with tree-shaded backyards. The Barrett House was torn down in 1940.

9/ Tennessee Williams

400 W. 43rd St. between Ninth and Tenth Avenue.

This huge apartment complex called **Manhattan Plaza** was opened in 1977 in one of Manhattan's sleazier neighborhoods. Built as a federally subsidized residence mainly for members of New York's performing arts community, it houses 3,000 residents, 70 percent of them theater people. Williams moved here in 1978 and stayed for three years, but he found the place too noisy and lived much of the time at the **Hotel Elysee** on East 54th Street. It was there that he died in 1983 (see Section Two, Tour 1, Number 15).

10/ Lucky Luciano, D.W. Grifith

162 W. 44th St. at Broadway (southeast corner).

The **Hotel Claridge**, long ago replaced by this modern office building, once stood on this spot. Luciano, when he was becoming the leader of New York's organized crime in the 1920's, made this a center for his operations.

Griffith, still the most prominent American film director in 1919, stayed here that year waiting for his estate to be built outside New York City.

11/ The Lambs Club

130 W. 44th St. between Broadway and Sixth Avenue.

This is the building that houses the oldest theatrical club in New York. Opened in 1904, it was the meeting place and temporary residence of countless actors and entertainers over the years. Those who have lived here include **Al Jolson, John Barrymore, W.C. Fields, Spencer Tracy**, and **Bert Lahr.**

12/ Bix Beiderbecke

120 W. 44th St. between Broadway and Sixth Avenue.

The legendary jazz trumpeter moved into Room 605 in this old building in April 1930. It was then known as the **44th Street Hotel.** He made it his New York home while he performed with various bands in and out of the city. His alcoholism was killing him by then; he left here in 1931 to live in Queens where he died in a small apartment on August 6, 1931. He was 28 years old.

13/ David Belasco

111 W. 44th St. near Sixth Avenue.

In this theater built by and named for him in 1907, the famous Broadway producer lived in an elaborately furnished apartment above the auditorium. The theater was technically advanced for its time with a sophisticated lighting system, special effects studio, and an elevator stage.

14/ Hotel Astor

1515 Broadway at 44th Street (northwest corner).

Yet another famous New York hotel of the past, now gone, stood on this corner. The **Hotel Astor**, opened in 1904, and torn down in 1966 for this modern, 50-story office building, was one of the landmarks of **Times Square.** It was the residence of many famous New Yorkers, including **Monte Wooley, Carmen Miranda, Jimmy Durante, D.W. Griffith,** and **Arturo Toscanini.** So valued was Toscanini's patronage at the Astor that the management converted a bathroom into a kitchen so that his wife could cook his favorite foods. This corner where the old Astor stood has been renamed **One Astor Plaza.**

15/ Cary Grant

229 W. 46th St. between Broadway and Eighth Avenue.

In the mid-1920's, **Grant**---then known by his real name, **Archie Leach**---lived in a small room in this building which was the **National Vaudeville Artists Club.** He survived in those days working as a vaudeville acrobat, in a mind-reading stage act or at any small job he could get. His first acting chance came in a small role in the musical comedy, *Golden Dawn*, which opened on Broadway in 1927. Number 229 no longer exists; the building is now numbered 227 (the **Church of Scientology**).

16/ Hotel Edison

228 W. 47th St. between Broadway and Eighth Avenue.

This large, old hotel, once very popular with show business people, has been the home of many popular entertainers. Soon after their marriage in 1927, couples **George Burns** and **Gracie Allen** and **Jack Benny** and **Mary Livingstone** lived here for a few years. The Burnses lived on the ninth floor, the Bennys on the fourth.

Writer **Ring Lardner** was a very ill man when he spent part of the year of 1933 here, living in Room 1935. He later moved to East Hampton, Long Island where he died on September 25, 1933.

Playwright **Moss Hart** moved into a swank tower apartment here in 1931 soon after his play, *Once in a Lifetime*, co-written with **George S. Kaufman**, opened on Broadway.

17/ Harold Ross and Alexander Woollcott

412 W. 47th St. between Ninth and Tenth Avenue.

In 1922, **Ross** and wife **Jane Grant** purchased this house in the rough section of the city known as **Hell's Kitchen**. Soon joining them was *New York Times* writer **Alexander Woollcott** and a few other friends. They maintained separate apartments but shared communal dining and entertaining rooms. The house became a popular gathering place for New York artists, writers, and entertainers of the 1920's. While living here, Ross and Grant began to develop their plans for the creation of the *New Yorker* and their home served as a second office for the magazine in its first years. Housekeeping was broken up when feuding between Ross and Woollcott led to the latter's departure in 1927. Ross and Grant finally moved out upon their divorce in 1928.

18/ Hotel Forrest

224 W. 49th St. between Broadway and Eighth Avenue.

Now called the **Hotel Consulate**, the old Forrest was another hotel best known as a residence for entertainers who performed in the **Times Square-Broadway** district. Comedian **Bert Lahr** and his first wife, **Mercedes**, lived here in the mid-1920's while he worked the vaudeville circuit. At one time or another, it was the New York home to **Jack Benny, George Burns** and **Gracie Allen, Fred Allen**, and **Jack Haley**.

Journalist **Damon Runyon**, after separating from his wife and family in 1928, had bachelor quarters here until the late 1930's. The hotel stands next to the **Eugene O'Neill Theatre**.

19/ Lenny Bruce

155 W. 47th St. between Sixth and Seventh Avenue.

On this site where a parking ramp now stands, next to the scruffy **Hotel Ashley,** stood the run-down **Americana Hotel**. It was here that Bruce, the hip comedian of the 1950's and early 1960's lived whenever he was in New York City. The place was identified by Bruce's biographer **Albert**

Goldman as "one of the most bizarre hotels in the world: a combination whorehouse, opium den and lunatic asylum." The location is directly across the street from the **Palace Theater**.

20/ Coolidge Hotel
131 W. 47th St. between Sixth and Seventh Avenue.

A modern glass office building stands here now but 60 years ago, on this site, stood the **Coolidge Hotel**, largely occupied by entertainers. It was just down the block from the **Palace Theater** at 1564 Broadway (still operating today), the place that all entertainers dreamed of playing in those days.

In 1921, actress **Gracie Allen** lived here with a roommate named **Mary Kelly**. **George Burns** was dating Gracie then and trying to persuade her to team up with him. Burns' good friend **Jack Benny**, also a struggling vaudeville comedian, lived at the Coolidge, and fell in love with Mary Kelly. Benny and Burns both married in January 1927; Burns to Gracie Allen, Benny to **Mary Livingstone** after his romance with Mary Kelly fizzled.

The Coolidge Hotel resembled the **Hotel Rio**, which still stands across the street at 132 W. 47th

21/ Delmore Schwartz
70 W. 46th St. at Sixth Avenue (southeast corner).

In 1966, the **Columbia Hotel** stood on this site now occupied by the **1166 Avenue of the Americas Building**. On July 11 of that year, in Room 506 of that old hotel, the poet Schwartz died of a heart attack. He was 52.

22/ Irving Berlin
29 W. 46th St. between Fifth and Sixth Avenue.

The great songwriter lived in an apartment in this old building from 1922 until 1930. While living here, he wrote such standards as *"Always,"* *"Blue Skies,"* and *"Puttin on the Ritz."* He lived here as a bachelor until January 1926 when he married his second wife, **Ellin Mackay.** They moved to larger quarters in 1930.

Section Two:

Midtown East of Fifth Avenue

17 Beekman Place

Home of Irving Berlin

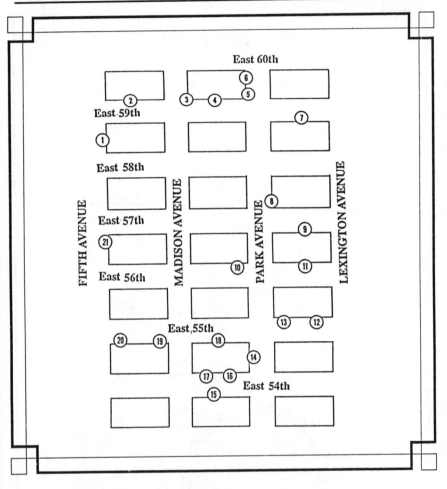

Tour 1

1/ Savoy Plaza Hotel
2/ Piet Mondrian
3/ Polly Adler
4/ Edward Hopper
5/ Hotel Delmonico
6/ Philip Barry
7/ Stieglitz-O'Keeffe
8/ William Randolph Hearst
9/ Bertolt Brecht
10/ Lillian Gish
11/ Hotel Lombardy

12/ Montgomery Clift
13/ John O'Hara
14/ George S. Kaufman
15/ Hotel Elysee
16/ Stieglitz-O'Keeffe
17/ Lillian Russell
18/ Steve Allen
19/ Polly Adler
20/ St. Regis Hotel
21/ Cole Porter

Section Two:

Midtown East of Fifth Avenue

Midtown East of Fifth Avenue *stretches from* **East 42nd Street** *to* **East 60th Street** *and between* **Fifth Avenue** *and the* **East River.** *Like Midtown West, this section can be divided roughly into two areas. The* **first,** *between* **Fifth Avenue** *and* **Third Avenue,** *was once largely a neighborhood of big mansions and brownstones. As the wealthiest New Yorkers moved uptown between the Civil War and the turn of the century, they made lower Fifth Avenue (south of Central Park) the original Millionaires' Row. Today, almost all of these palaces are gone, replaced for the most part by modern commercial office buildings. The* **second** *area, between* **Third Avenue** *and the* **East River,** *was once mainly a section of middle class homes and working class tenements. It has retained its residential character, although the homes of the poor along the river have been replaced by luxury buildings. This area contains such wonderful neighborhoods as* **Turtle Bay, Beekman Place,** *and* **Sutton Place.** **Midtown East** *was home for a number of important New Yorkers and, although much of it has been radically altered, many of their residences are still standing.*

Tour 1

1/ Savoy Plaza Hotel
767 Fifth Ave. between 58th and 59th Street.

The mammoth **General Motors Building** stands here now but this was once the site of the 30-story **Savoy Plaza Hotel**, one of Manhattan's most beautiful and luxurious hotels. Built in 1927, it was the New York home of a number of celebrities, especially movie people. Actors **William Powell, Joan Crawford** and **Zsa Zsa Gabor** all lived here. Paramount Studios mogul **Adolph Zukor** made the hotel his New York headquarters. The Savoy was demolished in 1965.

2/ Piet Mondrian
15 E. 59th St. near Fifth Avenue.

The great Dutch modernist painter spent the last four months of his life in a fourth-floor apartment on this site. He had moved here in October, 1943, after living on East 56th Street for three years (see this section, Tour 2, Number 12). He died on February 1, 1944, at the nearby **Murray Hill Hospital**. This office building which replaced his apartment is just next to the rear of the **Sherry Netherland Hotel** and across the street from the **General Motors Building.**

3/ Polly Adler
Corner of 59th Street and Madison Avenue.

New York's most famous "madam" maintained one of her most famous brothels in the 1920's on this corner. She described it as very old, with paper-thin walls and creaking floors. It became a rendezvous for many celebrities and members of the Social Register.

4/ Edward Hopper
53 E. 59th St. between Madison and Park Avenue.

Hopper was a young and unknown artist in the first decade of the century when he lived in a studio at this address. Success was a long time coming for him; at the famous *Armory Show* of 1913, he managed to sell his first painting but he didn't sell another for ten years. Hopper moved to Greenwich Village in 1913 and made it his New York home for the rest of his life (See Section Eight, Tour 2, Number 1). His studio here at 59th Street has long been replaced by office condominiums.

5/ Ed Sullivan and Lorenz Hart
502 Park Ave. at 59th Street (northwest corner).

This 32-two story building was known for years as the **Hotel Delmonico**. **Sullivan**, the newspaper columnist and television variety show host, lived here on the 11th floor from 1944 until his death in 1973. **Lorenz Hart**, the lyricist of the **Rodgers and Hart** team, made this building his residence in the last year of his life. He was found unconscious in his apartment here on November 17, 1943, and died in a hospital a few days later. The building is now a cooperative and has been renamed **Delmonico's**.

6/ Philip Barry
510 Park Ave. at 60th Street (southwest corner).

The playwright who wrote *The Philadelphia Story* and *Holiday* moved to this apartment building in 1948. He died here of a heart attack in December, 1949, at age 53.

7/ Alfred Stieglitz and Georgia O'Keeffe
114 E. 59th St. between Park and Lexington Avenue.

In July 1918, **Stieglitz** separated from his first wife, Emmeline, and moved into a studio on this site with painter **Georgia O'Keeffe**. They lived and worked here together until the end of 1920. It wasn't until 1924 that they were married. This site is next door to the **Argosy Book Store**.

8/ William Randolph Hearst and Marion Davies
465 Park Ave. at 57th St. (northeast corner).

This elegant 42-story apartment building is the **Ritz Tower**, which opened its doors in 1927. **Hearst**, the millionaire journalist, bought it in 1928 and maintained a large suite here which he often stayed in with his longtime mistress, actress **Marion Davies**, when they were not in California. Hearst was forced to sell the building in 1938 when his newspaper empire began to erode. The **Ritz Tower** has always attracted celebrities; others who have lived here include actresses **Greta Garbo** and **Paulette Goddard**.

9/ Bertolt Brecht
124 E. 57th St. between Park and Lexington Avenue.

The German playwright, in exile from his country during the war, was living with his family in Los Angeles in 1943. In February of that year, he traveled to New York to visit his mistress, **Ruth Berlau**, who was renting a fourth-floor apartment in this building He stayed here with her for four months, spending his time visiting fellow exiles, lecturing, and working on a play. Brecht continued to make California his American home until he finally returned to Europe for good in 1947.

10/ Lillian Gish
444 Park Ave. at 56th Street.

The silent screen actress lived at this residential hotel called the **Drake** from 1946 to 1949.

11/ Hotel Lombardy
111 E. 56th St. between Park and Lexington Avenue.

This famous residential hotel has been the home of many famous New Yorkers. **Ernest Hemingway** lived here for a short time in 1941, just after his marriage to his third wife, **Martha Gellhorn**. Broadway composer **Richard Rodgers** had an apartment on the 19th floor in 1929 and 1930 before and after his marriage to his wife, Dorothy. **Edna Ferber** lived at the Lombardy from 1930 to 1935 and wrote *Dinner at Eight* with **George S. Kaufman** while here. This was **George Burns** and **Gracie Allen's** last Manhattan home before moving to Hollywood in 1935. **Sinclair Lewis** lived alone here after his marriage to **Dorothy Thompson**. in 1939-40. **Henry Fonda** made this his residence in 1947 while he starred in *Mr. Roberts* on Broadway.

12/ Montgomery Clift
127 E. 55th St. between Park and Lexington Avenue.

Clift was 24 and acting in small roles in the New York theater when he moved out of his parents' home and took a small sublet walk-up above a laundromat on this site in 1944. For the first year, he continued to eat dinners with his parents and would sometimes move back with them when he got tired of taking care of himself. The place was shabby and practically unfurnished. Clift continued to live in this $40 a month flat even when he became famous. He finally left it in 1951 for a more spacious place uptown (see Section Three, Tour 2, Number 11).

13/ John O'Hara
103 E. 55th St. at Park Avenue.

In 1935, the writer, already famous after the recent publication of his first novel, *Appointment in Samarra,* lived on the ground floor of an apartment on this site where the **Chemical Bank Building** now stands. Among the conveniences of this establishment, according to biographer **Matthew Bruccoli**, were a butler and a thriving brothel across the street. **O'Hara** began to write his novel *Butterfield 8* while he lived here. He was 29 years old.

14/ George S. Kaufman
410 Park Ave. between 54th and 55th Street.

Between 1943 and 1949, the playwright and Broadway director occupied a townhouse here where a **Chase Manhattan Bank** now stands. It was here in 1945 that his wife, **Beatrice**, died. Kaufman's only major Broadway success during this period was *Born Yesterday* which opened in 1946. In May, 1949, he married for the second time to 35-year-old actress ,**Leueen MacGrath**.

15/ Hotel Elysee
56-60 E. 54th St. between Madison and Park Avenue.

The **Elysee** has been a popular home for Manhattan celebrities over the years. **Joe DiMaggio** had a suite here in the 1950's whenever he was staying in New York.

This was **Tallulah Bankhead's** favorite hotel; she was here from 1931 until 1938.

Dashiell Hammett, broke and trying to write, lived at the Elysee in 1931. Soon after Hammett met **Lillian Hellman**, they stayed here together for a time and Hellman lived here alone in the late 1930's.

Ring Lardner had a short residency. **Ethel Barrymore** made this her home

for a period in the 1930's. The Elysee was **Tennessee Williams'** last residence. He was found dead in his room here on February 24, 1983.

16/ Alfred Stieglitz and Georgia O'Keeffe
59 E. 54th St. between Madison and Park Avenue.

This was the photographer's last residence in New York. He and **O'Keeffe** moved into a small apartment in this building in October, 1942, and it was here on July 10, 1946, that he suffered the stroke that took his life three days later. The apartment was only a block away from his last studio, which was located on the 17th floor of the office building at 509 Madison Avenue at 53rd Street (southeast corner).

17/ Lillian Russell
57 E. 54th St. between Madison and Park Avenue.

The famous singer-actress of the Gay Nineties lived in this old building during the 1880's. Fittingly, the **Gay Nineties Cafe** is located on the ground floor here.

18/ Steve Allen
56 E. 55th St. between Madison and Park Avenue.

The versatile television personality and onetime host of the *Tonight Show* lived here in the early 50's, across from the **Friar's Club**.

Russell

that latter year the house was destroyed by fire and the St. Regis was built here in 1904. Since then, this luxurious hotel has hosted hundreds of celebrities from all the world.

In the last years of his life, **Ernest Hemingway** and his wife stayed here frequently during their New York visits. Surrealist painter **Salvador Dali** lived here for over a decade. **John Lennon** and his wife, **Yoko Ono**, lived in suites at the St. Regis in 1971-72.

Others who considered the St. Regis their favorite hotel include **Alfred Hitchcock, Rex Harrison, Humphrey Bogart**, and **John Huston**. The **St. Regis** closed in 1988 for extensive renovations to its interior.

19/ Polly Adler
30 E. 55th St. between Fifth Avenue and Madison Avenue (southwest corner).

Polly Adler was probably New York's most famous "madam." She lived and maintained one of her brothels here in the mid-1930's---a nine-room apartment on the second floor which rented for $225 a month. The building has been replaced by the **Sterling National Bank**.

20/ St. Regis Hotel
2 E. 55th St. at Fifth Avenue.

The elegant **St. Regis**, built by **Colonel John Jacob Astor**, has been called the "best European hotel in the United States."

It stands on the site of the mansion where journalist millionaire **Joseph Pulitzer** lived from 1887 to 1900. In

21/ Cole Porter
735 Fifth Avenue at 57th Street (southeast corner).

During the 1920's, the songwriter and his wife, **Linda Lee Thomas**, lived in an apartment on this spot, where **Tiffany's** and the **Manufacturer's Hanover Trust** building now stand.

He was living here in 1923 when he received news that he was inheriting a large fortune on the death of his grandfather. He used the money to rent luxurious villas in Venice during the following three years.

After the success of his musical, *Fifty Million Frenchmen,* in 1929, Cole and Linda took up residence in Paris and New York--spending six months in one place, six months in the other.

They moved to the **Waldorf-Astoria** in 1935. **Tiffany's** moved to this corner in 1940.

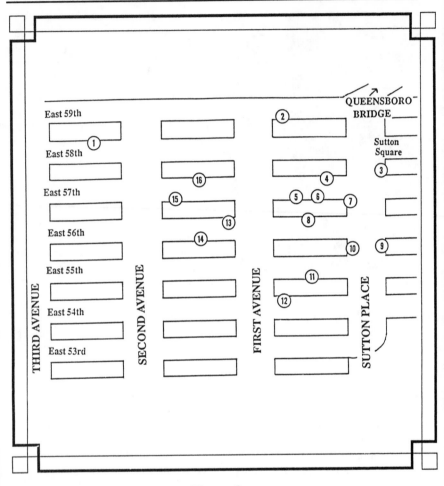

Tour 2

1/ Tennessee Williams
2/ John Cheever
3/ J. Paul Getty
4/ Tallulah Bankhead
5/ Lillian Gish
6/ Marilyn Monroe
7/ William Saroyan
8/ Jerome Kern

9/ Robert Sherwood
10/ Joan Crawford
11/ Noel Coward
12/ Stieglitz-O'Keeffe
13/ Piet Mondrian
14/ Sutton Club Hotel
15/ J.D. Salinger
16/ Ogden Nash

Tour 2

1/ Tennessee Williams
235 E. 58th St. between Second and Third Avenue.

He moved into an apartment in this attractive three-story white brick building in 1948 and stayed until the early 50's. His plays, *Summer and Smoke and The Rose Tattoo*, opened on Broadway during that time.

2/ John Cheever
400 E. 59th St. at First Avenue.

The writer moved into this brick apartment building with his wife and young daughter in the late 1940's. Their living room windows looked directly out at the Queensboro Bridge across the street. **Cheever** was becoming successful by this time with regularly featured stories in the *New Yorker*. The noise of traffic on the bridge finally drove the Cheevers out of the city in 1951 when they moved to a country house in Scarborough, New York.

3/ J. Paul Getty
1 Sutton Place at 57th Street (northeast corner).

Sutton Place continues to be one of New York's most prestigious streets. **Getty** moved into this four-level neo-Georgian townhouse in the mid-1930's, fleeing from the publicity in Los Angeles surrounding his divorce from his fourth wife, Ann. It was at this time that Getty became interested in fine art and antiques and began collecting objects for his new home on a grand scale.

It became a passion that dominated his private life until his death.

4/ Tallulah Bankhead
447 E. 57th St. between First Avenue and Sutton Place.

The actress was 60 years old and in poor health when she moved into a five-room condominium on the 13th floor of this building in 1962. She spent the last six years of her life here and died in nearby **St. Luke's Hospital** in December, 1968.

5/ Lillian Gish
430 E. 57th St. between First Avenue and Sutton Place.

The actress lived here for many years beginning in the early 1950's. Her mother had an apartment in the same building. In her autobiography, **Gish** said that "the **Sutton Place** area is home to me. I have lived in the neighborhood since 1929 and it is like a village where everyone knows you."

6/ Marilyn Monroe and Arthur Miller
444 E. 57th St. between First Avenue and Sutton Place.

They rented a large apartment on the 13th floor of this building in 1956, soon after their marriage. It was here that Miller wrote the final draft of *The Misfits*. They made this their New York home until their divorce in 1961. Miller moved back to his old home in the **Chel-**

sea Hotel, but Marilyn continued to live here until her death. She died in Los Angeles in August, 1962.

7/ William Saroyan
2 Sutton Place S. at 57th Street (southwest corner).

T he author lived here with his wife, Carol, in the 1940's. It was his last New York residence. Entertainer **George Jessel** also lived at this address. Across the street at **3 Sutton Place South** is the residence of the **Secretary-General of the United Nations.**

8/ Jerome Kern
411 E. 56th St. between First Avenue and Sutton Place.

T he Broadway musical composer was born in a house on this site (where modern apartments now stand) in 1885. He lived here until the age of five.

9/ Robert Sherwood
25 Sutton Place S. between 55th and 56th Street.

T he playwright lived in a house on this site from the early 1940's until his death in 1955. While he lived here, he wrote *There Shall Be No Night* (1941) and *Roosevelt and Hopkins* (1949), both of which won **Pulitzer Prizes**. The modern high-rise standing here today was built in 1959.

10/ Joan Crawford
36 Sutton Place S. between 55th and 56th Street.

T he actress was 47 years old in 1955 when she married businessman **Alfred Steele** and moved into his luxury eight-room apartment here. They stayed until 1957.

11/ Noel Coward
404 E. 55th St. between First Avenue and Sutton Place.

T his was the playwright's last Manhattan residence. He died in 1973 in Jamaica.

12/ Alfred Stieglitz and Georgia O'Keeffe
405 E. 54th St. at First Avenue.

S tieglitz and **O'Keeffe** rented a penthouse in this building in the fall of 1936. He was 72 years old. The apartment, with a beautiful view of the Queensboro Bridge and the East River, was simply furnished with Navajo artifacts brought from New Mexico by O'Keeffe. The couple lived here until October 1942.

13/ Piet Mondrian
353 E. 56th St. at First Avenue.

M ondrian moved from London to the United States in October, 1940, and his first home in New York was a tiny apartment on this site. (Number 353 is gone, replaced by Number 345.) It was located on the third floor facing First Avenue, across the street

Stieglitz

The **Sutton Club** had been built to accommodate a women's club, but when the deal fell through, it was converted into a hotel. Because the occupancy rate was low, West was able to offer rooms to his literary friends at reduced rates. During a difficult time in their careers, a long list of famous writers stayed here. They include **Erskine Caldwell, S.J. Perelman, Edmund Wilson**, and **James T. Farrell..**

Dashiell Hammett and **Lillian Hellman** moved into a tiny suite of three rooms here in the fall of 1932, and it was here that he wrote his last novel, *The Thin Man.*

15/ J. D. Salinger
300 E. 57th St. at Second Avenue.

He rented a small apartment here in 1951, soon after the publication of his novel, *Catcher in the Rye*, made him famous. The place was extremely bare; it was furnished with only a lamp and an artist's drawing board. On the wall was one picture of himself in uniform. **Salinger** lived here until the end of 1952 when he moved permanently to New Hampshire.

Writer **Stephen Vincent Benet** lived in a house on a site just east of here, at 326 E. 57th St. in the late 1920's.

16/ Ogden Nash
333 E. 57th St. between First and Second Avenue.

Nash, famous as American's best known producer of humorous poetry, lived in this building from 1956 until the early 1960's. He died in Baltimore in 1971.

from the **Sutton Club Hotel**. The painter loved Manhattan, especially the skyscrapers which he regarded as a kind of blueprint of the city of the future. Some of his greatest work was done here. He moved to a different apartment in 1943 (see this section, Tour 1, Number 2).

14/ Sutton Club Hotel
330 E. 56th St. between First and Second Avenue.

This hotel has become a literary landmark of sorts. **Nathaniel West** supported himself as the night manager here in the 1930's while he struggled to complete his novel *Miss Lonelyhearts.*

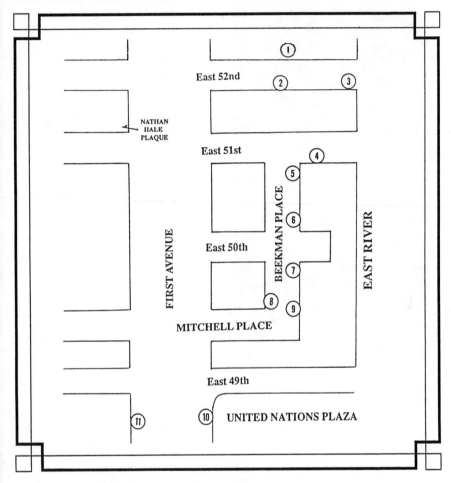

Tour 3

1/ **River House**
2/ **Humphrey Bogart**
3/ **The Campanile**
4/ **Max Ernst**
5/ **Billy Rose**
6/ **Katharine Cornell**

7/ **Irving Berlin**
8/ **Greta Garbo**
9/ **John D. Rockefeller III**
10/ **Truman Capote**
11/ **Thomas Wolfe**

Tour 3

1/ River House
435 E. 52nd St. at the East River.

This 26-story apartment house is one of the most luxurious in the world. It was opened in 1931 and its name became immediately synonymous with wealth and privilege.

Time Magazine publisher **Henry Luce** and his second wife, **Clare Boothe Luce**, took a 15-room apartment here in 1935 after their wedding and stayed until 1938 when they moved to the **Waldorf Astoria. Marshall Field, Cornelius Vanderbilt Whitney, Josh Logan**, and **Angier Biddle Duke** have also lived here.

2/ Humphrey Bogart
434 E. 52nd St. between First Avenue and the East River.

He moved into this house in the early 1930's with his second wife, **Mary Philips.** He was living here when he starred in the Broadway play, *The Petrified Forest*, in 1935. It was the role of **Duke Mantee** in this play that made him famous. He left for Hollywood in 1936 to begin his movie career.

3/ The Campanile
450 E. 52nd St. at the East River.

Completed in 1930, this is, like its neighbor the **River House** across the street, one of New York's most famous apartment houses. Among its well-known residents was **Alexander Woollcott**, who entertained his **Algonquin Round Table** companions in his third floor apartment here from 1927 until 1936. His friend, **Dorothy Parker**, dubbed the place "wit's end."

Actress **Greta Garbo** made this her home for many years. Other famous residents were **Noel Coward** and **Ralph Pulitzer.**

4/ Max Ernst and Peggy Guggenheim
440 E. 51st St. at the East River.

Ernst, the great German Surrealist painter, and **Guggenheim**, the wealthy art collector and patron to artists, had met in Europe. They returned to New York together in 1941 after the Nazi occupation and she leased this beautiful town house on the East River. The place was called **Hale House** because it was thought to be the spot where patriot **Nathan Hale** was hanged during the American Revolution (see Nathan Hale plaque on the building at the northwest corner of East 51st Street and First Avenue).

Ernst had his studio on the third floor. **Guggenheim** hung her collection of Surrealist and abstract paintings in the living room. Ernst covered the place with Indian artifacts from the Pacific Northwest and the American Southwest. Ernst and Guggenheim were married in December, 1941, but their time together at Hale House was troubled and they separated in 1943. Ernst left New York permanently in 1946 to live in Arizona. He returned to Paris in 1951.

Beekman Place

This quiet, elegant enclave tucked between **First Avenue** *and the* **East River** *from* **49th** Street *to* **51st Street**, *has been an attraction for prominent New Yorkers since the American Revolution. As you walk south, starting at* **51st Street**, *you will see the homes of the following people (numbers 5-9):*

5/ Billy Rose
33 Beekman Place at 51st Street.

The Broadway producer moved into this house with his second wife, **Eleanor**, after their marriage in 1939. The place had 14 rooms on five floors and was filled with expensive paintings and antiques. **Rose** lived here until 1951 when he was forced to leave by a court order obtained by his wife during their divorce contest. He moved to his apartment in the **Ziegfeld Theater**. Rose and Eleanor were divorced in 1952.

6/ Katharine Cornell
23 Beekman Place near 50th Street.

The stage actress moved into this five-story house overlooking the Hudson River in 1921 soon after her marriage to director **Guthrie Mc-Clintic**. They lived here for 31 years until 1952. During that period **Cornell** gained fame in a string of roles, the most famous being her portrayal of **Elizabeth** in *The Barretts of Wimpole Street* which she performed over a thousand times. She died in 1974 at age 81.

7/ Irving Berlin
17 Beekman Place at 50th Street.

This town house is the last New York home of the great American songwriter. **Berlin** lived here with his wife, novelist **Ellin Mackay**, for over three decades. The Berlins were married for 62 years. Mrs. Berlin suffered a stroke while she was living here and died at age 85 in 1988.

8/ Greta Garbo
2 Beekman Place at Mitchell Place.

The legendary movie actress had a six-room apartment here in the 1930's. She was at the height of her popularity at the time. This apartment was her New York home when she wasn't in Hollywood.

9/ John D. Rockefeller 3rd
1 Beekman Place at Mitchell Place.

The philanthropist grandson of the founder of **Standard Oil Company** lived here from 1934 until his death in an auto collision in 1978. During that period, he was director of **Rockefeller Center** and president of the **Rockefeller Foundation.**

John Marquand, the novelist who wrote *The Late George Apley*, lived at the same address for many years. Rockefeller was his brother-in-law. **Noel Coward** also lived here in 1933.

10/ Truman Capote
870 United Nations Plaza (First Avenue between 48th and 49th Streets).

Capote moved into a large apartment on the 22nd floor of this building overlooking the East River in 1965, just before his novel, *In Cold Blood*, was published. He lived here until his death in 1984. He died in Los Angeles.

11/ Thomas Wolfe
865 First Ave. between 48th and 49th Street

Wolfe had just turned 35 and was already a successful novelist in September, 1935, when he moved into a three-room apartment here, directly across the street from **870 United Nations Plaza**. The apartment, on the 14th floor, was just a short two blocks away from the home of his editor **Maxwell Perkins** (This section, Tour 4, Number 6) and Wolfe visited him there frequently during this period. Wolfe lived here until September, 1937.

Tour 4

1/ John Steinbeck
330 E. 51st St. between First and Second Avenue.

Soon after his marriage to **Gwyndolyn Conger** in the summer of 1943, **Steinbeck** moved into the lower part of this three-story brick house. At that time, he was working as a war correspondent for the *New York Herald Tribune* and spent some months in Europe. A son was born to him here in 1944 and, that summer, he spent time writing his novel, *Cannery Row*. The Steinbecks moved out in the fall of 1944.

2/ John O'Hara
230 E. 51st St. between Second and Third Avenue.

The 27-year-old writer lived in a room here at this small hotel called the **Pickwick Arms** in 1933 and 1934, paying eight dollars a week. He was broke but not starving.

It was here that he wrote the novel that made him famous, *Appointment in Samarra*. He would start writing at midnight and worked through the early hours of the morning, typing on his bed since his room was too small for a desk. When his work was done, he slept until noon and spent the afternoons at the movies, visiting **Dorothy Parker**, or playing backgammon at **Ira Gershwin's** East 72nd Street apartment.

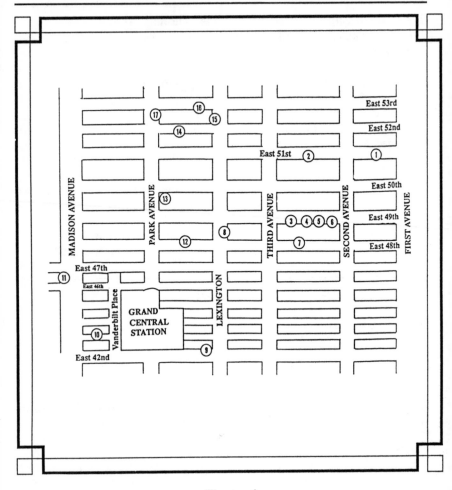

Tour 4

1/ John Steinbeck
2/ John O'Hara
3/ Henry Luce
4/ Ruth Gordon
5/ Katharine Hepburn
6/ Maxwell Perkins
7/ E.B. White
8/ Stieglitz-O'Keeffe
9/ F. Scott Fitzgerald

10/ F. Scott Fitzgerald
11/ Ritz-Carlton Hotel
12/ Ernest Hemingway
13/ Waldorf-Astoria Towers
14/ Gloria Swanson
15/ Marilyn Monroe
16/ Montgomery Clift
17/ Harold Arlen

Turtle Bay Gardens

The quiet block encompassing **48th** *and* **49th Streets** *between* **Second** *and* **Third** *Avenue is known as* **Turtle Bay Gardens**. *It is made up mainly of picturesque row houses, back to back, dating from the 1860's. They share a common garden running through the middle of the block, invisible from the street. This neighborhood has attracted many prominent New Yorkers over the years, including* **Mary Martin, Judge Learned Hand** *and* **Leopold Stokowski**. *Other residents with their houses are listed below (numbers* **3-7**).

3/ Henry Luce
234 E. 49th St.

In 1927, the magazine publisher, with his first wife, **Lila**, moved into this town house with Italian fountains in its backyard garden. His *Time Magazine*, started in 1923, was just beginning to turn profitable. *Time's* offices were only a few blocks away at 25 W. 45th St., and **Luce** walked to work there every morning in 15 minutes.

4/ Ruth Gordon and Garson Kanin
242 E. 49th St.

The actress and her screenwriter husband lived here for many years. In 1954, they leased the house to actor **Tyrone Power** for a brief period while he performed in a Broadway play.

5/ Katharine Hepburn
244 E. 49th St.

Hepburn rented this house in 1932 while she was appearing in a Broadway play called *The Warrior's Husband*.

Later she bought the house and lived here for over 50 years. It was also in 1932 that she began her movie career when she starred in *A Bill of Divorcement* opposite **John Barrymore**.

6/ Maxwell Perkins
246 E. 49th St.

This was the home of the famed editor at Charles Scribner's Sons, who nurtured such famous writers as **F. Scott Fitzgerald, Ernest Hemingway**, and **Thomas Wolfe**. He moved here in 1932 from New Canaan, Connecticut, and stayed until 1938.

7/ E.B.White and Katharine Angell White
229 E. 48th St.

The New Yorker's most famous essayist leased an apartment here with his wife, editor **Katharine Angell White**, in 1946. (Earlier, he lived at numbers 245 and 239 on this block). They spent their summers in Maine and made this place their winter home for the next 11 years. White was living here when he wrote *Charlotte's Web* in 1949. In 1957 the Whites moved permanently to their home in Maine.

8/ Alfred Stieglitz and Georgia O'Keeffe
525 Lexington Ave. between 48th and 49th Street.

After their marriage in 1924, they moved into Suite 3003 of this hotel, then called the **Hotel Shelton**. They made it their New York home for the next 10 years. The living room faced north and east with a wonderful view of the city skyline; O'Keeffe used it as her studio. This hotel is now called **Halloran House**.

9/ F. Scott and Zelda Fitzgerald
109 E. 42nd St. at Lexington Avenue.

It's now the glass-covered **Grand Hyatt**, but when **Scott** and **Zelda** moved here in May 1920 soon after their wedding, it was the **Commodore Hotel**. They had just been booted out of the **Biltmore Hotel** (see Number 10 below). It was here that they spent half an hour spinning in the revolving door. They were soon turned out for disturbing the other guests.

10/ F. Scott and Zelda Fitzgerald
43 E. 43rd St. between Madison Avenue and Vanderbilt Place.

Fitzgerald moved into the **Biltmore Hotel** on this site in March, 1920, after the publication of his first novel, *This Side of Paradise*. **Zelda** came from Montgomery, Alabama, a few days later, and after their wedding at **St. Patrick's Cathedral** on April 3, 1920, they stayed here for their honeymoon in suite 2109. Their exuberant lifestyle disturbed the manage-ment and they were asked to leave within a month. The Biltmore stood until 1981 when it was razed for the present **Bank of America Plaza**.

11/ Ritz-Carlton Hotel
374 Madison Ave. at 46th Street (northwest corner.)

One of the landmark luxury hotels of this century, the old **Ritz-Carlton** stood on this site for 41 years. Opened in 1910, it was the stopping place for many prominent people and a few made it their residence.

Al Jolson always kept a suite there in the 1920's. New Yorker editor **Harold Ross** lived there as a bachelor after his divorce from **Jane Grant** in the early 1930's. Gambler and underworld king **Arnold Rothstein** lived in a deluxe suite there in the mid-twenties.

The Ritz-Carlton was demolished in 1951. A **Chase Bank** office stands here today.

12/ Ernest Hemingway
111 E. 48th St. between Park and Lexington Avenue

This building was once the **Hotel Barclay** and it was a favorite **Hemingway** New York hotel. He stayed here in 1937 while he finished his novel, *To Have and Have Not*. In July, 1940, he worked on revision of *For Whom the Bell Tolls* here, delivering his book piecemeal by runner to his publisher (*Scribners*) which was located a few blocks away. **Eugene O'Neill** and his wife, **Carlotta**, also lived here for seven months in 1945-46.

13/ Waldorf-Astoria Towers
100 E. 50th St. (southeast corner of Park Avenue).

The 112 luxury suites of the **Waldorf Towers**, reached by this separate entrance, just around the corner from the great hotel's main lobby on Park Avenue, are world-famous. The **Towers,** opened in 1931, occupies the 27th through 42nd floors of the hotel. They have been the home of numerous prominent New Yorkers. Fifty-one units are leased on a permanent basis; the other 61 are transient apartments.

Porter

Cole Porter lived in a suite on the 41st floor from 1935 until 1964 with his wife, Linda. They had adjacent but separate apartments. Porter had "acoustical mud" placed in the walls to deaden the piano sounds so that he wouldn't disturb his neighbors late at night. He also installed his own parquet floor from an old French chateau.

In later years, **Frank Sinatra** made this same suite his New York home.

General Douglas MacArthur spent his last years at the Towers. He moved there with his wife in 1951 after he was relieved of his command in Japan. He lived in Suite 37A until his death in 1964.

Charles (Lucky Luciano), the king of organized crime, resided at the Waldorf from 1933 until 1936, when prosecutor **Thomas Dewey** sent him to prison. He stayed in Suite 39D under the alias of Charles Ross, and paid $800 a month in rent.

Former President **Herbert Hoover** spent the last 25 years of his life here, in Suite 31A. He died in 1964.

Suite 42A has been the home of American ambassadors to the United Nations: **Henry Cabot Lodge** lived here in the 1950's; **Adlai Stevenson** was here from 1961 until his death in 1965. **Henry Luce** and his wife **Clare Booth Luce** moved here in 1938 and stayed for many years. Other famous residents have been **Spencer Tracy, Joseph Kennedy, Moss Hart, Elsa Maxwell**, and the **Duke and Duchess of Windsor.**

14/ Gloria Swanson
114 E. 52nd St. between Park and Lexington Avenue.

The **Gladstone Hotel** stood on this site for many years. The film actress rented a string of three suites here in the 1920's and made them her Manhattan home. She split her time between New York and Hollywood.

15/ Marilyn Monroe
Lexington Avenue and East 52nd Street (northwest corner)

It was on this spot one night in September, 1954, (in front of the **Trans Lux** movie theater, since demolished) that the famous scene from the movie, *The Seven Year Itch*, was filmed. It is, of course, the one in which the draft from the subway vent blew **Monroe's** skirt high in the air. It was witnessed by a few thousand onlookers. The subway vent is still here.

16/ Montgomery Clift
116 E. 53rd St. between Park and Lexington Avenue.

Clift was a teenager when he moved with his family into a high-rise apartment on this site next to the YWCA in 1935. (The apartment has been replaced by the **Seagram's Building**.) In that year, the young actor performed in his first role on Broadway at the age of 14. He continued to act on the New York stage over the next several years while still living here with his parents. He finally moved to his own apartment in 1943 (see this section, Tour 1, Number 12). He made his first appearance in the movies in 1948.

17/ Harold Arlen
375 Park Ave. between 52nd and 53rd Street (southeast corner).

The composer of such popular songs as *"Stormy Weather," "That Old Black Magic,"* and *"Over the Rainbow"* lived in a huge penthouse apartment here in the 1940's. It has been replaced by the **Seagram Building**.

Section Three:

The Upper East Side

157 E. 69th Street

Studio of Mark Rothko

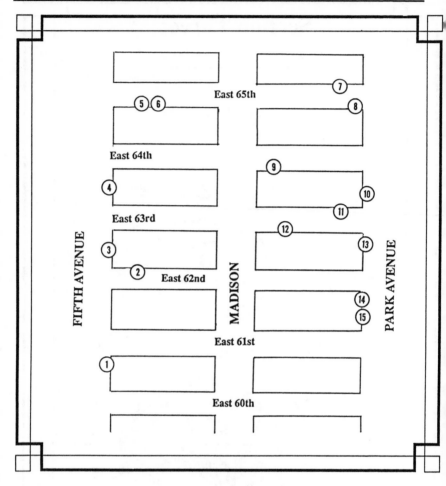

Tour 1

1/ Hotel Pierre
2/ Ernest Hemingway
3/ Nelson Rockefeller
4/ Al Smith
5/ Moss Hart
6/ James J. Hill
7/ Franklin D. Roosevelt
8/ Jimmy Walker

9/ Charles Evans Hughes
10/ Edward R. Murrow
11/ Maxfield Parrish
12/ The Lowell
13/ Willa Cather
14/ Danny Kaye
15/ Eddie Rickenbacker

Section Three:

The Upper East Side

Since the turn of the century, the **Upper East Side** has been the favorite residential area of Manhattan's wealthiest people. Its borders, as defined for our purposes, run from **East 59th Street** to **East 100th Street**, and between **Fifth Avenue** and the **East River**.

The most famous section of the Upper East Side runs along **Fifth Avenue** and its related side streets, from the **Sherry Netherland Hotel** at 59th Street to the **Carnegie** mansion at 91st. Here, along the eastern border of **Central Park**, are found block after block of the spectacular marble and brownstone houses that gave this stretch its name, **Millionaires' Row**. Most of these homes were built between 1900 and 1930 by the industrial tycoons and their followers who amassed their fortunes in the era after the Civil War. Now far too costly to be maintained by a single family, most of these residences have either been subdivided into cooperatives or taken over by various learned societies, clubs, museums and foreign delegations.

The area east of **Millionaires' Row** was divided into two distinct neighborhoods at the turn of the century, both containing different populations. The **first**, spanning Madison, Park and Lexington Avenues, was basically middle class in composition. The **second**, which ran from Lexington to the East River, was a working class tenement neighborhood with a concentration of ethnic families of German, Irish, Italian, Czech, and Eastern European origin.

Both of these two areas have greatly changed in character since those days. After the First World War, middle class **Park Avenue** became a new magnet for the affluent, and that famous street quickly became a name synonymous with the rich as luxury high-rise apartment buildings were constructed, divided into elegant duplexes and triplexes. In the last 25 years, the working class streets closer to the river have been transformed into an upper middle class neighborhood as tenements and brownstones have either been renovated or torn down to make way for the many large modern apartments seen here today.

The **Upper East Side** has had a rich and varied history. It has been and continues to be, the home of a great number of New York's most famous people.

Tour 1

1/ Hotel Pierre
799 Fifth Ave. between 60th and 61st Street.

Built in 1928, it is still one of New York's most elegant hotels. In 1938 it was losing money when **J. Paul Getty** bought it and, as a member of Manhattan's smart set, was able to attract his playmates and their friends to its facilities.

From then on, its reputation was fixed. It was heiress **Barbara Hutton's** favorite New York residence when she wasn't living in California or Europe. She had suites on the 36th and later the 39th floor.

Dashiell Hammett, the detective novelist of *Maltese Falcon* fame, started writing *The Thin Man* here in 1932 and, in September of that year, having run up a bill he could not cover, he disguised himself by wearing several layers of clothing and left without paying.

In 1938, while broke and coming off a drinking bout, **John O'Hara** wrote the first *Pal Joey* story (one of fourteen) here which later became the **Rodgers and Hart** musical.

The French film director **Rene Clair** lived here in 1940 after escaping the German Occupation.

Actors **Robert Taylor** and **Barbara Stanwyck** made the Pierre their New York home during the 1940's. They were divorced in 1952.

2/ Ernest Hemingway
1 E. 62nd St. near Fifth Avenue.

In the fall of 1959, the writer, wanting a place that would insure him of privacy when he came to New York, rented a fourth-floor apartment here across from the **Knickerbocker Club**. **Hemingway** was in poor physical and mental condition at the time. During the summer of 1960, he set up a card table in the corner of the living room to serve as an office but could do little writing. He left New York for good soon after. He died in July, 1961, at his home in Ketchum, Idaho.

3/ Nelson Rockefeller
810 and 812 Fifth Ave. between 62nd and 63rd Street.

Rockefeller, with his first wife, **Mary**, moved into a large apartment here at 810 Fifth Ave. in 1931. They made it their New York home for many years; he was living here when he became governor in 1958. He moved out in 1961 when he fell in love with **Margaretta "Happy" Murphy**. After his divorce from his first wife, Rockefeller and Happy were married in 1963 and they lived together in a large triplex apartment at 812 Fifth Ave. until his death in 1979.

4/ Al Smith, Herbert Lehman
820 Fifth Ave. between 63rd and 64th Street.

Smith, former New York governor and Democratic candidate for presi-

Roosevelt

this building in the early 1940's. He was living here in 1946 when he married actress **Kitty Carlisle**.

6/ James J. Hill
8 E. 65th St. near Fifth Avenue.

Hill, the man who built the transcontinental **Great Northern Railroad** (now the **Burlington Northern**), completed in 1893, made this mansion his New York home from 1906 until his death in 1916. Hill's home base was St. Paul, Minnesota. This building, numbered 6 through 12, now houses the **Pakistani Mission** to the **United Nations**.

7/ Franklin & Eleanor Roosevelt
49 E. 65th St. between Madison and Park Avenue.

This brick and limestone townhouse was built in 1907 by **Sara Delano Roosevelt** as a wedding present for her newly wedded son and his wife. The mother lived next door in No. 47, and **Franklin** and **Eleanor** moved into No. 49 in the fall of 1908 and stayed until he was elected to the State Legislature in Albany in 1910. They continued to live here off and on over the next 20 years, and it was in the fourth floor front bedroom that Franklin began his convalescence from the polio attack that almost ended his career.

dent in 1928, moved to a large apartment here in the late 1930's. He was a great animal lover and enjoyed spending time across the street at the **Central Park Zoo** where he was made an honorary member of the staff. Smith died while living here in October of 1944.

Lehman, New York's Democratic governor from 1933 to 1942, made this his Manhattan residence when he was not in Albany. He later became a U.S. senator.

5/ Moss Hart
4 E. 65th St. near Fifth Avenue.

The Broadway director and playwright was a bachelor when he moved into a large duplex apartment in

8/ Jimmy Walker
610 Park Ave. at 65th Street (entrance on 65th St.).

New York's flamboyant and notorious mayor from 1925 to

1932 moved to a suite here in 1928, soon after leaving his wife, Janet, for showgirl **Betty Compton**. (It was called the **Mayfair** then; now it's the **Mayfair Regent Hotel**.) He lived here until 1932 when, amid accusations of corruption, he was forced to resign his office. He immediately left for Europe, where he married Betty Compton and lived for the next three years.

9/ Charles Evans Hughes
32 E. 64th St. at Madison Avenue.

Hughes, a former New York governor, lived in this brick building from 1917 until 1921. He moved here soon after he had lost the 1916 presidential election to **Woodrow Wilson**. He returned to his private law practice. Later Hughes would become U.S. Secretary of State and Chief Justice of the Supreme Court.

10/ Edward R. Murrow
580 Park Ave. between 63rd and 64th Street.

CBS radio and television's famous journalist and newsbroadcaster had an apartment in this huge building from 1946 until 1961. He left New York for Washington in 1961 to head the **U.S. Information Agency**. He died in 1965.

11/ Maxfield Parrish
49 E. 63rd St. between Madison and Park Avenue.

The artist was 48 years old and already famous when he spent the winter of 1918-19 painting here in this beautiful white stone building with the below-street-level entrance. **Parrish**

was married but he enjoyed spending his winters alone with his work; his wife usually stayed in Georgia during the cold months. Parrish died at his longtime home in Cornish, New Hampshire in 1966.

12/ The Lowell (Apartments)
28 E. 63rd St. between Madison and Park Avenue.

In 1970, the *New York Times* political columnist **Walter Lippmann**, then 81 years old, moved into an apartment in this residential Art Deco hotel. He lived here with his wife until 1973 when he suffered a heart attack. He died in a nursing home in December 1974. Writer **Dorothy Parker** lived in this same hotel in 1931.

13/ Willa Cather
570 Park Ave. at 63rd Street.

The author of *O Pioneers!* and *My Antonia* moved into a large apartment in the rear of this building with her lifetime companion, **Edith Lewis**, in the fall of 1932. It was her last New York residence. She died of a cerebral hemorrhage here on the afternoon of April 24, 1947.

14/ Danny Kaye
550 Park Ave. between 61st and 62nd Street.

The comedian rented a 10-room apartment here in the early 1940's soon after his marriage to **Sylvia Fine**. **Kaye** also owned a home in Hollywood but made this building his New York residence for a number of years.

15/ Eddie Rickenbacker
540 Park Ave. between 61st and 62nd Street.

The World War I flying hero lived here at the **Regency Hotel** in the 1950's and 60's.

Tour 2

1/ Ray Bolger
123 E. 62nd St. between Park and Lexington Avenue.

After his memorable performance as the scarecrow in **The Wizard of Oz** in 1939, **Bolger** returned to New York to appear in a Broadway musical called *Keep Off the Grass*. He lived in this house during that period. Bolger continued to act on both the stage and screen throughout the 1940's.

2/ Charles Evans Hughes
129 E. 62nd St. between Park and Lexington Avenue.

The future New York governor, Republican presidential candidate, and Supreme Court justice moved into this three-story house with his new bride, **Antoinette Carter**, in December 1888. He had just entered a law partnership with her father. Hughes' parents lived with them in this house--the rent was $1,200 a year. A year later, after the birth of their son, they moved to Brooklyn.

3/ Bennett Cerf
132 E. 62nd St. between Park and Lexington Avenue.

This five-story gray house was the residence of the **Random House** publisher and his wife, Phyllis, from 1941 until his death in 1971.

4/ Otto Preminger
129 E. 64th St. near Lexington Avenue.

The movie director who made such films as *Exodus* and *The Man With the Golden Arm* lived in this white stucco building. He died here of cancer in 1986.

5/ Barbizon Hotel
140 E. 63rd St. (S.E. corner of Lexington and 63rd).

This 22-story red brick building was once a residence hotel for women only, usually those with wealthy parents. It was built in 1927.

Grace Kelly lived here for two years in 1947-48 while she studied acting at the American Academy of Dramatic Arts.

Sylvia Plath stayed here in 1953 when she was a *Mademoiselle* magazine

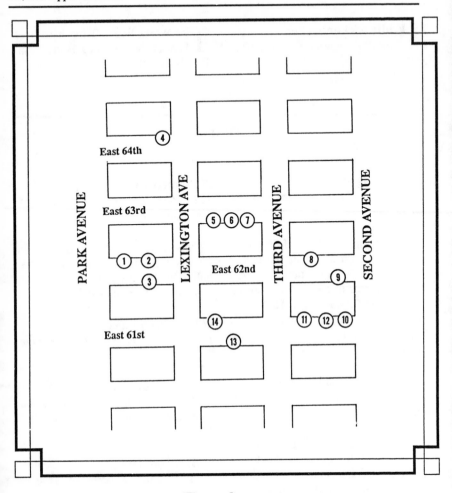

Tour 2

1/ Ray Bolger
2/ Charles Evans Hughes
3/ Bennett Cerf
4/ Otto Preminger
5/ Barbizon Hotel
6/ Gypsy Rose Lee
7/ George S. Kaufman

8/ Eleanor Roosevelt
9/ Tallulah Bankhead
10/ Walter Lippmann
11/ Montgomery Clift
12/ Montgomery Clift
13/ The Seven Year Itch
14/ Oscar Hammerstein II

Kaufman

guest editor from Smith College and she fictionalized the hotel as the **Amazon** in her book, *The Bell Jar.*

Actresses **Gene Tierney** and **Nanette Fabray** also lived here.

6/ Gypsy Rose Lee
154 E. 63rd St. between Lexington and Third Avenue.

T he *Queen of Burlesque* moved to this 24-room white stucco house in the early 1940's. The house, elaborately designed with 18th century French interiors, originally cost $300,000 to build. **Lee** lived here up to the last year of her life. She moved to Beverly Hills, California, in 1970 where she died of cancer at the age of 56.

7/ George S. Kaufman
158 E. 63rd between Lexington and Third Avenue.

T he humorist, Broadway director, and playwright lived in a penthouse apartment here with his wife, **Beatrice,** from 1929 until 1932. Earlier it was the home of playgirl **Peggy Hopkins Joyce.** While he lived here, **Kaufman** co-authored four hit Broadway plays including *Once in a Lifetime, The Band Wagon, Of Thee I Sing,* and *Dinner at Eight.*

8/ Eleanor Roosevelt
211 E. 62nd St. between Third and Second Avenue

F.D.R.'s widow was 68 years old when she moved from a suite at the **Park Sheraton Hotel** to an apartment in this brick duplex in 1953. She needed more space; this larger apartment had a garden and allowed her to bring her dog into town from her regular home in Hyde Park. **Mrs. Roosevelt** moved out of this place in 1958 after she purchased a house on 55 E. 74th St. (see this section, Tour Four, Number 12).

9/ Tallulah Bankhead
230 E. 62nd St. between Third and Second Avenue.

I n 1956, the actress bought this four-story townhouse. It had 12 rooms, six fireplaces, a latticed garden, and sycamore trees. **Tallulah** was becoming increasingly dependent on alcohol and drugs at this period of her life and finding it difficult to get dramatic roles. She sold this place to millionaire **Hun-**

tington **Hartford** at a handsome profit and moved out in 1962.

10/ Walter Lippmann
245 E. 61st St. between Third and Second Avenue.

From 1929 to 1937, **Lippmann** lived in this house with a walk-down entrance and the brown oval door with his first wife. He moved out when they were divorced. Lippmann moved to Washington, D.C., soon afterward and spent nearly 30 years there as the *New York Times* political analyst.

11/ Montgomery Clift
209 E. 61st St. between Third and Second Avenue.

In 1951, the actor was an established star when he gave up his $40-a-month walk-up at 127 E. 55th St . for a spacious duplex apartment in this building.

Clift was becoming drug-dependent at this time and built a 14-foot long medicine cabinet in his bathroom filled with drugs. He was forced to leave this apartment in 1960 after it was severely damaged by fire.

He moved a few doors up the block to 217 E. 61st St. (see below).

12/ Montgomery Clift
217 E. 61st St. between Third and Second Avenue.

He purchased this spacious, four-story brownstone in January of 1960. It contained seven rooms, six fireplaces, six baths, and a large tree-filled garden.

It was the same home that **Theodore Roosevelt** had given to his daughter, **Alice Longworth**, for her wedding. Critic **Clifton Fadiman** had lived here in the 1940's.

This turned out to be Clift's last home. He died here of a heart attack on the morning of July 23, 1966. He was only 45 years old.

13/ The "Seven Year Itch" Apartment
164 E. 61st St. between Third and Lexington Avenue.

This is the brownstone apartment building where the characters played by **Marilyn Monroe** and **Tom Ewell** lived in the 1954 motion picture.

14/ Oscar Hammerstein II
157 E. 61st St. between Third and Lexington Avenue.

The lyricist who collaborated with **Richard Rodgers** on many Broadway musicals rented an apartment here in the 1940's. He maintained his primary residence at a farm in Pennsylvania. During the years he stayed here, he worked on *Oklahoma* and *Carousel*.

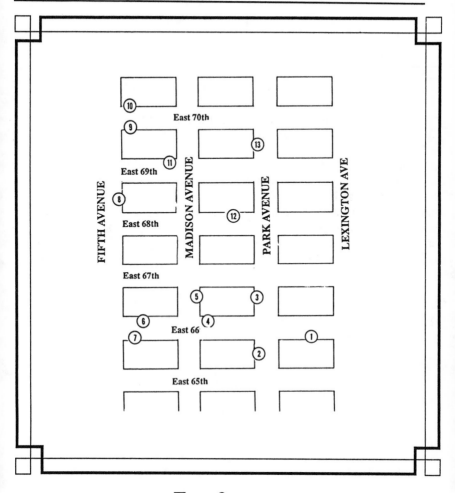

Tour 3

1/ Isak Dinesen
2/ Artur Rubinstein
3/ Henry Fonda
4/ Boris Karloff
5/ Walter Lippmann
6/ Dashiell Hammett
7/ Bernard Baruch

8/ Gertrude Vanderbilt Whitney
9/ Joan Crawford
10/ Henry Clay Frick
11/ Fanny Brice
12/ Dorothy Kilgallen
13/ Dave Garroway

Tour 3

1/ Isak Dinesen
122 E. 66th St. between Park and Lexington Avenue.

The Danish author of **Out of Africa** was 73 years old when she arrived in New York in January, 1959, for a lecture and readings tour. For much of the time during her visit, she stayed here at the **Cosmopolitan Club**, where she was made an honorary member. Near the end of her visit, she collapsed from exhaustion and nearly died. She returned to Denmark in April, 1959.

2/ Artur Rubinstein, Lillian Hellman
630 Park Ave. at 66th Street.

The world-famous pianist lived here from 1956 until 1972 when he moved to France. He died in Switzerland in 1982 at age 95. Hellman moved into a tenth-floor apartment here in 1970 and it was her principal residence until her death in 1984.

Dorothy Kilgallen also lived in this building.

3/ Henry Fonda
650 Park Ave. between 66th and 67th Street.

Fonda had recently made the successful transition from stage to movies in 1936 when he married his second wife, socialite **Frances Brokaw**.

They stayed in her apartment in this building for a brief period after their wedding. At that time, the place was called the **Sulgrave Hotel.** They soon moved to Hollywood.

4/ Boris Karloff
45 E. 66th St. at Madison Avenue.

The actor who became famous for his screen portrayal of the monster in *Frankenstein* lived in this large brick apartment house in the 1940's. He was performing in the popular Broadway play, *Arsenic and Old Lace*, which ran for 1,444 performances from 1941 until 1944.

5/ Walter Lippmann
785 Madison Ave. between 66th and 67th Street.

The political analyst took an apartment here with his first wife, **Faye,** in 1919 after they had returned from the Versailles peace conference in France. He wrote for the *New Republic* until 1922, when he became an editorial writer for the *New York World*. The Lippmanns stayed here until 1923, then moved to Greenwich Village.

6/ Dashiell Hammett
15 E. 66th St. near Fifth Avenue.

After his discharge from the U.S. Army in 1945, the detective writer took an apartment in this building. He was 51 years old. He divided his time between here and **Lillian Hellman's** farm in Westchester, New York. By then, Hammett was struggling with a serious alcohol problem and had given up writing completely. He moved to Greenwich Village in 1947.

7/ Bernard Baruch
4 E. 66th St. near Fifth Avenue.

T he multi-millionaire financier and advisor to many U.S. presidents lived in a six-room apartment here from 1946 until his death. He died of a heart attack here on June 20, 1965. He was 94 years old.

8/ Gertrude Vanderbilt Whitney
871 Fifth Ave. between 68th and 69th Street.

T he aunt of **Gloria Vanderbilt**, she won custody of the ten-year old girl from **Gloria Morgan Vanderbilt**, the child's mother, in a celebrated court case in 1934.

Her mansion where young Gloria lived with her in the 1930's was demolished in 1942 after her death and replaced by this 45-story apartment building.

9/ Joan Crawford
2 E. 70th St. at Fifth Avenue.

T he movie actress lived in a huge penthouse condominium here with her last husband, soft-drink executive **Alfred Steele**, from 1957 until 1959. Its 16 rooms had cost nearly $1 million to remodel.

One writer said that **Crawford's** fetish for cleanliness extended even to the flowers and plants, which were plastic so that they could be regularly washed in soapy water. Visitors were not allowed to wear shoes beyond the entrance hall because Crawford didn't want her pure white rugs soiled.

10/ Henry Clay Frick
1 E. 70th St. at Fifth Avenue.

T he millionaire steel magnate and partner of **Andrew Carnegie** was 65 years old when he moved to New York from Pittsburgh in 1914 to live in this elegant mansion.

Frick had gained national attention in 1892 when he was badly wounded but survived an assassination attempt on his life by anarchist **Alexander Berkman** after Frick had ruthlessly crushed a steelworkers strike at Homestead, Pennsylvania.

He built this mansion not only as his residence but to house his large collection of European art. He died in 1919. After his wife's death in 1935, the house was converted into the public museum, the **Frick Collection**.

11/ Fanny Brice and Billy Rose
15 E. 69th St. at Madison Avenue.

T he musical comedy star took an apartment in this building (now the **Westbury Hotel**) with her children in the late 1920's, after her divorce from **Nicky Arnstein**. She lived here with **Billy Rose**, her third husband, after their wedding in February, 1929.

They stayed together until their divorce in 1938--the same year that Fanny moved permanently to California.

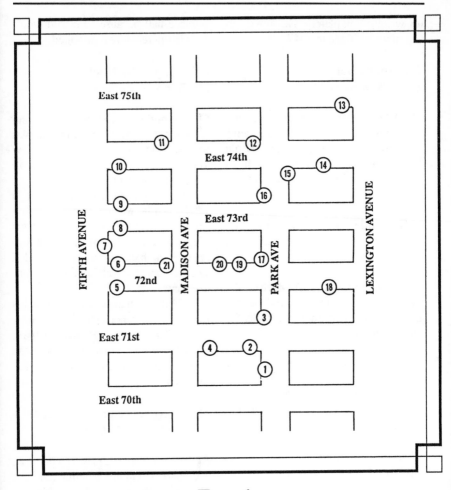

Tour 4

1/ Edna Ferber
2/ Richard Rodgers
3/ John D. Rockefeller Jr.
4/ David Sarnoff
5/ Henry Luce
6/ Joseph Pulitzer
7/ Arnold Rothstein
8/ Gloria Swanson
9/ Joseph Pulitzer
10/ Marc Chagall
11/ Dorothy Parker

12/ Eleanor Roosevelt
13/ Lunt and Fontanne
14/ Jerome Kern
15/ Edna Ferber
16/ Dag Hammarskjold
17/ Tyrone Power
18/ George Gershwin
19/ Gloria Vanderbilt
20/ Teilhard de Chardin
21/ Charles Tiffany

12/ Dorothy Kilgallen

45 E. 68th St. between Madison and Park Avenue.

This five-story apartment house was the gossip columnist's last home. She died in her sleep here on November 8, 1965, at age 52.

13/ Dave Garroway

710 Park Ave. between 69th and 70th Street.

Morning television's **Garroway** lived in this apartment building during the years that he was the original host of NBC's **Today Show**, from 1952 until 1961.

Tour 4

1/ Edna Ferber

730 Park Ave. between 70th and 71st St. (entrance on 71st Street).

The novelist and playwright moved to a six-room apartment in this building in 1950 and lived here until her death in 1968, at the age of 83. She wrote her popular novel, *Giant*, while she lived here.

2/ Richard Rodgers

70 E. 71st St. at Park Avenue.

The composer of many Broadway musical scores lived in this huge co-op building (same as 730 Park Avenue; see Number 1 above) with his wife, **Dorothy**, from 1945 until 1971. It was the period when he collaborated with **Oscar Hammerstein II** on such hits as *South Pacific, The King and I,* and *The Sound of Music*.

3/ John D. Rockefeller, Jr.

740 Park Ave. at 71st Street.

The only son of the founder of the **Standard Oil Company** and father of **John III, Nelson, Laurance, Winthrop**, and **David Rockefeller**, was 62 years old in 1936 when he moved to a large penthouse apartment here. By that time, Rockefeller had distinguished himself by directing large amounts of the Rockefeller fortune towards philanthropic causes. He lived here until his death in 1960.

4/ David Sarnoff

44 E. 71st St. between Madison and Park Avenue.

The radio and television broadcasting pioneer lived in this six-story 30-room townhouse for many years. **Sarnoff**, who rose from a $5.50-a-week office boy to chairman of the **RCA Corporation** and later **NBC**, died here in December 1971 at the age of 80.

5/ Henry Luce
4 E. 72nd St. at Fifth Avenue.

In 1932, **Luce**, whose *Time* Magazine was enjoying a great success, moved to a large apartment here with his first wife, **Lila**, and their two sons. He moved away in 1935 when he fell in love with **Clare Boothe**. Luce and Boothe were married soon after his divorce from Lila.

6 / Joseph Pulitzer
9 E. 72nd St. near Fifth Avenue.

The famed newspaper publisher leased this house, called the **Sloane Mansion**, from 1900 until 1904, after his home on East 55th Street burned down. It is now the **Lycee Francais de New York**. **Pulitzer** moved one block north to his new home in 1904 (see number 9 below).

7/ Arnold Rothstein
912 Fifth Ave. between 72nd and 73rd Street.

The notorious gambler and underworld kingpin, best known as the man who fixed the **World Series of 1919**, lived here with his wife, Carolyn, during the last few years of his life. It was his residence in November, 1928, when he was murdered at the **Park Central Hotel**. He was 46 years old. The killer was never found.

Pulitzer

8/ Gloria Swanson
920 Fifth Ave. at 73rd Street.

The film star moved into a large apartment here in 1938. It was her principal residence for the rest of her life. By the late 1930's, her movie career had faded and she became a successful businesswoman. In 1950, she made a spectacular film comeback in *Sunset Boulevard*, for which she won an **Academy Award**. She died while living at this address in 1983 at the age of 84.

9/ Joseph Pulitzer
11 E. 73rd St. near Fifth Avenue.

Designed by **Stanford White**, this huge Italian Renaissance mansion was built by the publisher in 1904 to replace his home on East 55th Street, which was destroyed by fire in 1900. **Pulitzer** directed White to make the house fireproof, a rare phenomenon at the turn of the century. Pulitzer lived here until his death in 1911.

10/ Marc Chagall
4 E. 74th St. near Fifth Avenue.

The painter, with his wife, **Bella**, rented an apartment here in September, 1941, soon after they had fled the Nazi occupation in France. Feeling homesick, they decorated the walls of their place with Chagall's paintings to create the illusion of being back in Paris. After Bella's death in 1944, Chagall's daughter persuaded him to move into her large apartment at 75 Riverside Drive (see Section Four, Tour 4, Number 3).

11/ Dorothy Parker
23 E. 74th St. near Madison Avenue.

This former residence hotel called the **Volney**, built in the 1920's, was writer **Dorothy Parker's** home for the last 15 years of her life. She was discovered dead of a heart attack in her rooms here on June 7, 1967.

Composer **Richard Rodgers** lived here in 1945. It is now a co-op apartment building.

12/ Eleanor Roosevelt
55 E. 74th St. near Park Avenue.

Mrs. Roosevelt was 75 years old when she purchased this house in 1958 with her close friend, **Dr. David Gurewitsch** and his wife. She moved into it in 1959 and it was her New York residence for the rest of her life. She died here on November 7, 1962.

13/ Alfred Lunt & Lynn Fontanne
130 E. 75th St. at Lexington Avenue.

The husband and wife stars of New York theater leased a luxury seven-room apartment in this building in 1936. They lived here until 1950, making this place the scene of some of the city's most elegant parties in that period.

14/ Jerome Kern
128 E. 74th St. between Park and Lexington Avenue.

The composer of popular songs lived in this four-story brownstone as a very young boy from 1890 until 1895. He probably learned to play the piano while he lived here.

15/ Edna Ferber
791 Park Ave. at 74th St. (southeast corner).

By the mid-1930's, she was a very successful novelist and playwright when she rented a large apartment in this building. Her mother, **Julia**, a constant companion throughout **Ferber's** life, moved in with her. The apartment, located on the 19th floor, had a huge outdoor terrace, big enough to play tennis on, and a lush garden complete with peach trees.

16/ Dag Hammarskjold
778 Park Ave. at 73rd Street.

The Swedish diplomat and **Secretary General** of the **United**

Nations from 1953 to 1961 made this large apartment his New York home.

17/ Tyrone Power
760 Park Ave. at 72nd Street.

T he actor was 40 years old when he rented a small, two-bedroom penthouse here in 1954. During this period, he appeared on Broadway in a play called *The Dark is Light Enough,* co-starring with **Katharine Cornell**.

18/ George Gershwin
132 E. 72nd St. near Lexington Avenue.

T he composer lived here from 1933 until 1936. It was his last New York home. His brother, **Ira**, lived across the street at 125 E. 72nd St. It was a huge 14-room apartment with an art studio and gymnasium and perhaps the largest private bar in New York. **Gershwin** had a direct telephone line to Ira's house so that they could be in instant creative contact. Gershwin began work on *Porgy and Bess* while he was here. He moved to California in 1936.

Ex-New York mayor **Jimmy Walker** and his second wife, showgirl **Betty Compton**, lived in this same building from 1935 until their divorce in 1941.

19/ Gloria Vanderbilt
49 E. 72nd St. between Madison and Park Avenue

G loria Morgan Vanderbilt rented a townhouse on this site from 1932 until 1936. She and her daughter, **Gloria**, lived in it until she lost custody of the child to **Gertrude Vanderbilt Whitney**, young Gloria's aunt, in 1934. A new apartment building, now renumbered 45, stands here today.

20/ Pierre Teilhard de Chardin
39 E. 72nd St. between Madison and Park Avenue.

T he Jesuit anthropologist and philosopher was visiting friends in an apartment here in 1955 when he died suddenly. He was 73 years old.

21/ Charles L. Tiffany
19 E. 72nd St. at Madison Avenue (northwest corner).

F rom 1885 until 1936, one of the earliest large New York City mansions stood on this corner. It was the gigantic Romanesque-style home of **Charles Tiffany**, the founder of the famous jewelry house. It was designed by architect **Stanford White**.

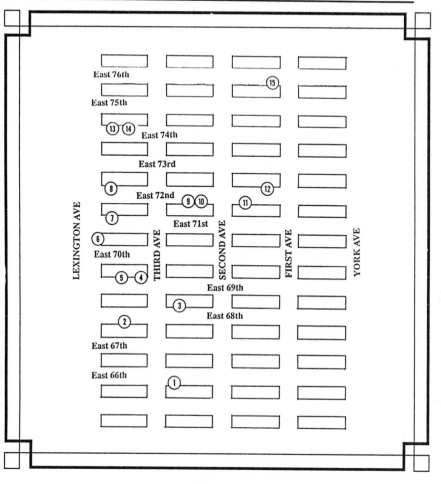

Tour 5

1/ Grace Kelly
2/ Joan Crawford
3/ Stephen Vincent Benet
4/ Rube Goldberg
5/ Mark Rothko
6/ Lunt and Fontanne
7/ Robert Sherwood
8/ Thomas Dewey

9/ John Steinbeck
10/ Elia Kazan
11/ Ethel Barrymore
12/ Diane Arbus
13/ Yul Brynner
14/ Elia Kazan
15/ Joe Namath

Tour 5

1/ Grace Kelly, Benny Goodman
200 E. 66th St. at Third Avenue.

This 20-story luxury apartment building, called **Manhattan House**, was built in 1950.

Grace Kelly moved here shortly after it opened and lived here until 1955. During that period she starred in such movies as *High Noon, Rear Window,* and *The Country Girl.* A biographer says that her apartment was unpretentious and often cluttered. Her only pet was a parakeet named Henry but she was seldom lonely; friends dropped by constantly to talk about acting and the theater.

Benny Goodman, one of the world's greatest jazz artists lived at Manhattan House for a number of years. He died of a heart attack here on June 13, 1986 at the age of 77.

2/ Joan Crawford
158 E. 68th St. between Lexington and Third Avenue.

This site, where buildings of **Hunter College** now stand, was the movie actress's last New York home. She died of a heart attack in her apartment here on May 10, 1977. During the last years of her life, she served as the first woman on the board of directors of **Pepsi Cola Company**. She worked as their major public relations spokesperson and official hostess.

3/ Stephen Vincent Benet
215 E. 68th St. near Third Avenue.

In the early 1940's, the **Pulitzer Prize**-winning writer lived in a house on the site where this modern apartment complex now stands. **Benet** was only 44 years old when he died in 1943.

4/ Rube Goldberg
169 E. 69th St. at Third Avenue (northwest corner).

This was the last home of **Goldberg**, the famous cartoonist and inventor of zany contraptions. He died here of cancer in 1970 at the age of 87.

5/ Mark Rothko
157 E. 69th St. between Lexington and Third Avenue.

This converted carriage house with huge black doors was the painter's last studio. He started to work here in 1964, finally leaving his family in 1969 to live here as well.

He experimented with the light by covering the skylight with a huge canvas parachute which he regulated with pulleys to give him the effects he wanted.

Rothko lived by himself in the studio for a year. It was here on February 25, 1970, that he committed suicide.

6/ Alfred Lunt and Lynn Fontanne

969 Lexington Ave. between 70th and 71st Street.

Soon after their wedding in May, 1922, the **Lunts** started married life in New York in a four-room unfurnished apartment on the second floor of this building. Just becoming famous in the theater, they lived here until 1925. After that, they lived in a series of hotels for 10 years until they settled into a permanent place in 1936 (see Tour 4, No. 13, this section).

7/ Robert Sherwood

153 E. 71st St. at Lexington Avenue.

The playwright who won four **Pulitzer Prizes** moved here in the early 1920's after his marriage to his first wife, **Mary Brandon**. He lived here until 1930 when they separated.

8/ Thomas Dewey

141 E. 72nd St. at Lexington Avenue.

This apartment building was the last New York residence of the former New York governor who lost two presidential elections. He lived here from 1955 until his death in 1971.

9/ John Steinbeck

206 E. 72nd St. between Second and Third Avenue.

Steinbeck lived in a beautiful brownstone house on this site from 1951 until his death in 1968. While here he wrote *Winter of Our Discontent* and *Travels with Charley* and won the **Nobel Prize** in 1962. The house was replaced by this modern apartment building called the **Wellesley**. Steinbeck's house was similar in appearance to the house still standing next door at 210 E. 72nd.

10/ Elia Kazan

212 E. 72nd St. between Second and Third Avenue.

Kazan, one of the few people to gain fame as a director of both stage and screen, lived here from 1955 until the early 1960's with his first wife, **Molly**. The house was close to his friend **John Steinbeck's** house at 206 E. 72nd.

While Kazan lived here, he directed *Cat on a Hot Tin Roof* and *Dark at the Top of the Stairs* for the stage and the movies *Baby Doll*, *A Face in the Crowd*, and *Splendor in the Grass.*

11/ Ethel Barrymore

320 E. 72nd St. between First and Second Avenue.

The actress was 61 years old in 1940 when she began performing in one of her most successful roles on the stage in *The Corn is Green.*

During that period she lived in an apartment in this brown brick building. She gave 461 performances on Broadway in the play before touring with it nationwide.

Barrymore moved permanently to California in 1945.

12/ Diane Arbus
319 E. 72nd St. between First and Second Avenue.

The photographer lived in a triplex here with her husband, **Allan**, between 1954 and 1958. The sculptor **Paul Manship** had lived in the place earlier. Number 319 is no longer an existing number: it is located between 315 and 325 East 72nd Street.

13/ Yul Brynner
151 E. 74th St. between Lexington and Third Avenue.

The actor rented this attractive four-story brick townhouse for many years. The house was owned by **Henry Fonda**.

14/ Elia Kazan
167 E. 74th St. between Lexington and Third Avenue.

The director of stage and film lived in this brownstone house with his first wife, **Molly**, and their four children from 1945 until 1955. His years here were perhaps the time of his greatest achievement. He directed the plays , *All My Sons, A Streetcar Named Desire,* and *Death of a Salesman,* and made movies of *Streetcar* as well as *Viva Zapata!* and *On the Waterfront.*

Barrymore

15/ Joe Namath
370 E. 76th St. near First Avenue.

During the late 1960's, when he was playing for the **New York Jets,** the star quarterback made his home in this modern high-rise apartment building called **Newport East**.

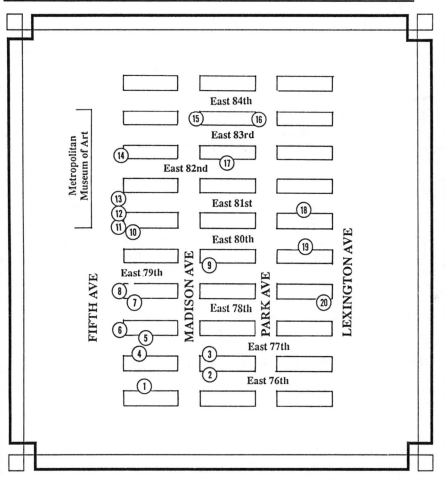

Tour 6

1/ Ethel Merman
2/ The Carlyle
3/ Richard Rodgers
4/ Gloria Vanderbilt
5/ George Balanchine
6/ Henry Luce
7/ James Duke
8/ John Hay Whitney
9/ Emily Post
10/ Arthur Hays Sulzberger

11/ Frank Woolworth
12/ George M. Cohan
13/ Charlie Parker
14/ Wendell Willkie
15/ Alfred Stieglitz
16/ Teilhard de Chardin
17/ Lillian Hellman
18/ Charles Evans Hughes
19/ Raymond Massey
20/ Irving Berlin

Tour 6

1/ Ethel Merman
20 E. 76th St. near Fifth Avenue.

The Broadway musical star lived in an apartment in this residential hotel called **The Surrey** during the last year of her life. She died here of a brain tumor in 1984 at the age of 76.

2/ The Carlyle
35 E. 76th St. near Madison Avenue.

The Carlyle, with its 38-story tower, is a New York landmark and one of its most elegant hotels. It was built in 1930 - 31 as an apartment hotel for wealthy tenants. This 76th Street entrance is for the transient guests who stay at the hotel temporarily; the tenant-owners' entrance (permanent residents) is on the opposite side of the building at 50 E. 77th St. (See Number 3 below). The Carlyle gained national attention when President **Harry Truman** began to stay here on his New York visits and was seen taking leisurely strolls in the neighborhood. President **John F. Kennedy** had a duplex suite here and frequently stopped in the 1960's. Writer **Ring Lardner** lived here briefly in the early 1930's, not long before his death.

3/ Richard Rodgers
50 E. 77th St. at Madison Avenue.

The Broadway composer moved into these **Carlyle Apartments** with his wife, **Dorothy**, after their return from Hollywood in 1933 and stayed until 1941. **Henry Ford II** and **Robert Sherwood** are among the other people who have lived in this exclusive residence, adjacent to the Hotel Carlyle.

4/ Gloria Vanderbilt
12 E. 77th St. near Fifth Avenue.

This was the home where Reginald Claypoole Vanderbilt, youngest son of **Cornelius Vanderbilt II**, and his young wife, **Gloria Morgan Vanderbilt**, were living when their daughter, **Gloria**, was born in 1924.

5/ George Balanchine
11 E. 77th St. near Fifth Avenue.

The choreographer and artistic director of the **New York City Ballet** moved into this beautiful house with the walk-down entrance in 1938 after his second marriage to dancer **Vera Zorina**. He lived here until the late 1940's.

His third wife, dancer **Maria Tallchief**, also lived here with him after he divorced Zorina.

6/ Henry Luce and Clare Boothe Luce
960 Fifth Ave. between 77th and 78th Street.

This was the last New York home of the *Time* Magazine publisher. He moved here to a large apartment in the 1960's with his wife, **Clare Boothe Luce**. It's directly across from Central Park, where Luce enjoyed taking long walks. He died at his western home in Phoenix, Arizona in 1967.

7/ James B. Duke
1 E. 78th St. at Fifth Avenue.

The tobacco millionaire, founder of the **American Tobacco Company**, built this white marble and sandstone mansion in 1912. He lived here until his death in 1925. In 1957, after the death of his widow, the house was donated to the **New York University's Institute of Fine Arts**.

8/ John Hay Whitney
972 Fifth Ave. between 78th and 79th Street.

The millionaire financier, sportsman, and ambassador made this his New York home for many years. In 1958, **Whitney** became the owner and publisher of one of New York's greatest newspapers, the *New York Herald Tribune*, which he operated until 1966 when it ran into financial difficulties and closed down. Whitney died in 1982. The building is now the **Cultural Service**, the **Embassy of France**.

9/ Emily Post
39 E. 79th St. at Madison Avenue.

The first lady of etiquette built this red brick apartment house in the early 1920's. She lived in it for nearly 40 years, surrounding herself with a circle of friends who lived rent-free in the other apartments in the building. Post died here in September, 1960, at the age of 86.

10/ Arthur Hays Sulzberger
5 E. 80th St. near Fifth Avenue.

Sulzberger was the president and publisher of the *New York Times* for more than 30 years. He lived here from 1928 until 1952. He became the head of the *Times* in 1935 after the death of his father-in-law, **Adolph Ochs**, who had been the owner since 1896. Sulzberger remained the publisher until 1961 when he turned the position over to his son, **Arthur Ochs Sulzberger**, the present publisher. The elder Sulzberger died in 1968.

11/ Frank W. Woolworth
990 Fifth Ave. at 80th Street.

This was the mansion owned by the *dimestore millionaire*. He moved here in 1901 and remained until his death in 1919. His granddaughter, **Barbara Hutton**, lived here with him as a young child after her mother **Edna Woolworth** committed suicide by jumping from a window at the **Plaza Hotel** in 1917. The residence here was sold by the family in the early 1920's during a period of financial decline. It is now the home of the **American-Irish Historical Society**.

12/ George M. Cohan
993 Fifth Ave. between 80th and 81st Street.

This house, across from the **Metropolitan Museum of Art**, was the Broadway star's last New York home. He moved here in the 1930's and died in his apartment of cancer on November 5, 1942. He was 64.

Cohan

13/ Charlie "Bird" Parker
995 Fifth Ave. at 81st Street.

T he immortal jazz saxophonist died here at the **Hotel Stanhope** on March 12, 1955. He had been visiting with a friend, the **Baroness Pannonica de Koenigswarter**, a wealthy eccentric who drove herself to jazz clubs in a silver Rolls Royce. Her apartment here at the Stanhope had become an elegant crash pad for a number of jazz musicians. Parker collapsed during his visit and died a few days later. He was only 34 years old.

14/ Wendell Willkie
1010 Fifth Ave. at 82nd Street.

T he man who ran against **Franklin Roosevelt** as the Republican candidate in 1940 lived in this house directly across from the entrance of the **Metropolitan Museum of Art** from 1929 until his death in 1944.

15/ Alfred Stieglitz
1111 Madison Ave. at 83rd Street.

T he photographer was 34 years old when he moved into this apartment building with his first wife, **Emmeline**, in 1898. He was still an artist without any financial resources and the rent was paid by his wife's annuities from her brother's business. Stieglitz moved away from here in 1918 when he fell in love with the young **Georgia O'Keeffe** (see Section Two, Tour 1, Number 7).

16/ Pierre Teilhard de Chardin
980 Park Ave. between 83rd and 84th Street.

T he controversial Jesuit philosopher lived in the rectory here of the **St. Ignatius Loyola Church** from 1951 until 1954. He died the year after leaving here.

17/ Lillian Hellman
63 E. 82nd St. between Madison and Park Avenue.

T he playwright author of *The Little Foxes* owned this beautiful four-story brick house with the blue doors from 1944 until 1970. **Dashiell Hammett** lived here with her on two different occasions. In 1948 she helped him to recover from illnesses caused by his alcoholism. In 1958, again in poor health, he came back here and remained in Hellman's care, financial and otherwise, for the final three years of his life. He died in 1961.

18/ Charles Evans Hughes
110 E. 81st St. between Park and Lexington Avenue.

T he famed New York governor, U.S. Secretary of State, Supreme Court Justice, and presidential candidate lived in a house on this site as a young man in 1886-88 when he began to practice law. The house has been replaced by a modern apartment building

19/ Raymond Massey
132 E. 80th St. between Park and Lexington Avenue.

T he stage and screen actor who was television's *"Dr. Kildare"* had an apartment here from the late 1930's until the early 1950's. He was living in this building in 1939 when he performed in the lead role that made him famous, *Abe Lincoln in Illinois,* written by **Robert Sherwood.**

20/ Irving Berlin
129 E. 78th St. near Lexington Avenue.

T he composer lived in this attractive brown house in the 1940's. It was his home during the period that he wrote the songs for such hit shows and movies as *Holiday Inn, This Is the Army,* and *Annie Get Your Gun.*

Tour 7

1/ Robert F. Wagner
244 E. 86th St. at Second Avenue.

N ew York's great Democratic U.S. senator lived in this red brick apartment building in the 1920's. This address is in the heart of the Manhattan neighborhood called **Yorkville,** which was the "Little Germany" of the early twentieth century. **Wagner,** born in the Rhineland, was Yorkville's most prominent public figure. He was a member of the **New York Supreme Court** from 1918 until 1926 while he lived at this address. In 1927 he began his first term as U.S. senator.

2/ Amy Vanderbilt
438 E. 87th St. between York and First Avenue.

T he famous socialite and world famous expert on etiquette owned this townhouse during the last years of her life. It was here on the night of December 27, 1974, that she fell to her death from a third floor window. She was 66 years old.

3/ Carl Schurz Park

T his pleasant urban park runs along the East River from 90th Street to Gracie Square at 84th Street. It is the

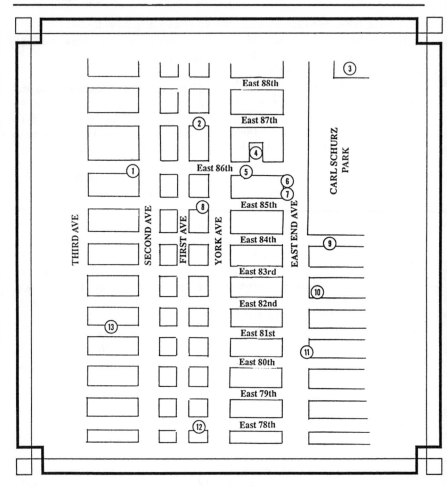

Tour 7

1/ Robert F. Wagner
2/ Amy Vanderbilt
3/ Gracie Mansion
4/ Henderson Place
5/ Robert F. Wagner
6/ Irving Berlin
7/ Jimmy Walker

8/ Henry Miller
9/ Gracie Square
10/ Robert Moses
11/ Ring Lardner
12/ James Cagney
13/ W.H. Auden

site of **Gracie Mansion**, a Federal-style country house built in 1799, that has served as the residence for New York mayors since 1942 when **Fiorello LaGuardia** moved in.

4/ Henderson Place
86th St. between York and East End Ave.(north side).

This neighborhood was once part of the country estate of **John Jacob Astor**. In 1882, a developer built 32 houses in this small enclave called **Henderson Place**. Now, only 24 of these three-story red brick Queen Anne style houses remain. Modern apartments on both sides have spoiled the original atmosphere but it's still a wonderful New York locale. Literary critic **Edmund Wilson** and his wife, novelist **Mary McCarthy** lived at 14 Henderson Place with their young son in 1944. It was just before they separated and divorced. Actors **Lynn Fontanne** and **Alfred Lunt** moved to a house here in 1950 and stayed for a number of years.

5/ Robert F. Wagner
530 E. 86th St. near East End Avenue.

Wagner, who served as New York's U.S. senator for over 20 years, lived in this Yorkville apartment across from **Henderson Place** from 1939 until his death in 1953. It was his New York home when he wasn't working in Washington. Wagner, a widower for many years, shared the residence with his son, **Robert F. Wagner, Jr.**, who later became the mayor of New York City.

6/ Irving Berlin
130 E. End Ave. at 86th Street (facing Carl Schurz Park).

Berlin lived in Apartment 16 of this large building during the 1930's with his wife, **Ellin Mackay**. His two youngest daughters were born while the Berlins lived here and during that period he wrote such songs as *"Easter Parade," "Cheek to Cheek,"* and *"I've Got My Love To Keep Me Warm."*

Aviation hero **Eddie Rickenbacker** also lived in this building during the 1940's, up to 1954.

7/ Jimmy Walker, George Balanchine
120 E. End Ave. at 85th Street (facing Carl Schurz Park).

This beautiful white stone building was the last home of the former mayor of New York. He moved here in 1945 with his two adopted children, his sister, and his two nephews. He was living here when he died on November 18, 1946.

Choreographer **George Balanchine** also lived in this building in the early 1940's with his wife, dancer **Vera Zorina**.

8/ Henry Miller
450 E. 85th St. at York Avenue.

The novelist who wrote *Tropic of Cancer* and *Tropic of Capricorn* was born on the top floor of this red brick building on December 26, 1891. His grandparents had emigrated from Germany and settled here in the neighborhood of **Yorkville** many years earlier. Miller's father was a tailor. The family moved to Brooklyn while Miller was still an infant.

9/ Gracie Square
84th St. between East End Ave. and the East River.

This short block is the southern border of **Carl Schurz Park**. The houses here have been the residences of many prominent New Yorkers. **Robert Moses** lived at Number 7 with his wife, **Mary**, from 1930 until 1939, during the time that he was becoming one of the most powerful government officials in the state's history.

Cornelia Otis Skinner lived at Number 7 in the 1940's. Number 10 was the home of **John Barrymore's** ex-wife **Michael Strange** and his daughter, **Diana Barrymore.** Journalist and critic **Alexander Woollcott** was living at that same address when he died in 1943. Number 10 was also the home of **Gloria Vanderbilt** and **Leopold Stokowski** during their marriage from 1945 to 1955.

10/ Robert Moses
1 Gracie Terrace (at 82nd Street between East End Ave. and the East River. Entrance at 75 E. End Ave.).

New York's master planner and builder and---working mainly behind the scenes---one of the most powerful and influential public figures in the history of the state, lived in a large apartment here from 1939 until his death in 1981. **Moses** occupied a number of New York state and city posts and played a major role in molding the

state's physical environment. During over 50 years of public service, he developed public works costing over *$27 billion,* including bridges, highways, playgrounds, parks, and public buildings. He died in 1981 at age 92.

11/ Ring Lardner
25 E. End Ave. at 80th St. (northeast corner).

In September, 1931, **Lardner** and his wife, **Ellis**, took an apartment in this 15-story apartment building called the

Lardner

Yorkgate. He had just come out of the hospital. His health continued to deteriorate and they were only able to remain at this address for six months before he was forced to return to the hospital. Lardner died in September, 1933, at the age of 48.

12/ James Cagney
420 E. 78th St. between York and First Avenue.

Cagney lived in an apartment in this four-story building as a teenager in 1917-1918. After his marriage to **Frances Willard Vernon** (his lifelong spouse) in September, 1922, the couple moved back here temporarily to live with his mother, **Carolyn**. Cagney was working as a young stage actor and dancer at that time.

13/ W. H. Auden
237 E. 81st St. between Third and Second Avenue.

The British poet moved to the U.S. with his friend, writer **Christopher Isherwood** in 1939. In April of that year, they rented a cheap apartment in this four-level brown building. Isherwood left for California in May where he lived for the rest of his life.

Auden stayed here until the middle of that year when he left on a cross-country tour. When he returned to New York in the fall of 1939, he moved to Brooklyn Heights.

Tour 8

1/ Robert F. Wagner
1327 Lexington Ave. between 88th and 89th Street.

The U.S. senator for New York lived in this huge brick apartment building (now renumbered 1311) from 1930 until 1939. He was a widower at that time and this place was his Manhattan home when he wasn't in Washington. **Wagner** was then at the height of his prominence as liberal New Deal lawmaker.

2/ Alexander Kerensky
109 E. 91st St. between Park and Lexington Avenue

The *man who ruled Russia* in 1917, before he was ousted by **Lenin** during the Bolshevik Revolution, lived in this five-story red-brick building.

He came to the U.S. in exile from Europe and lived on the top floor here from the mid-1940's until 1969. **Kerensky** died in 1970 at the age of 89.

3/ J.D. Salinger
1133 Park Ave at 91st Street.

The author of *Catcher in the Rye* was 13 years old in 1932 when he moved with his parents into this 15-story apartment building. After he flunked out of the **McBurney School** in Manhattan, he was sent to a military academy in Pennsylvania where he completed his high school education. **Salinger** served with the army in Europe during World War II, then returned here to live with his parents again and began his career as a writer. His first short stories appeared in the *New Yorker* in 1947.

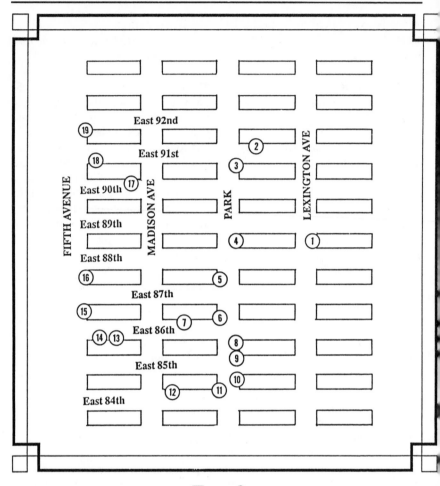

Tour 8

1/ Robert F. Wagner
2/ Alexander Kerensky
3/ J.D. Salinger
4/ Eugene O'Neill
5/ Truman Capote
6/ Conde Nast
7/ John O' Hara
8/ George S. Kaufman
9/ Walter Lippmann
10/ Steve Allen
11/ P.G. Wodehouse
12/ Eugene O'Neill
13/ Harold Arlen
14/ Otto Rank
15/ Bernard Baruch
16/ Oscar Hammerstein II
17/ Sinclair Lewis
18/ Andrew Carnegie
19/ E.F. Hutton

4/ Eugene O'Neill
1095 Park Ave. between 88th and 89th Street.

The playwright, with his second wife, **Carlotta**, leased an eight-room duplex apartment in this building in the fall of 1931. They had recently returned from France where they had lived for three years. While they lived here, his play, *Mourning Becomes Electra,* opened on the New York stage. O'Neill was unhappy living in New York; in the summer of 1932 they moved to a secluded home at Sea Island, Georgia.

5/ Truman Capote
1060 Park Ave. at 87th Street.

As a young writer, **Capote** lived here off and on during the 1940's in the apartment of his mother, **Nina**, and his stepfather. He worked on his novel, *Other Voices, Other Rooms,* while he stayed here.

6/ Conde Nast
1040 Park Ave. at 86th Street.

The millionaire magazine publisher of *Vogue, House and Garden*, and other popular publications, lived in a 30-room penthouse here from the early 1930's until his death in 1942. The apartment was a center of New York nightlife where socialites, Hollywood and Broadway celebrities, statesmen and royalty attended the elaborate dinners, dances and cocktail parties he gave. Amidst 18th century French paintings, Chinese screens and rococo splendor, **Nast** could entertain 100 cocktail guests on the roof, a dinner party of 50 downstairs, and another 200 in the ballroom, all at the same time.

7/ John O'Hara
55 E. 86th St. between Madison and Park Avenue.

O'Hara lived here from 1945 until 1949 in this 15-story brick apartment building. He wrote the novel, *A Rage to Live*, while he was here.

8/ George S. Kaufman
1035 Park Ave. at 86th Street.

Kaufman moved into this penthouse apartment with his second wife, **Leueen MacGrath**, in 1949, and they lived here until their divorce in 1957. He co-wrote the plays *The Solid Gold Cadillac* and *Silk Stockings* here. Kaufman lived here alone after the divorce; he died of a heart attack in the apartment on June 2, 1961. He was 71.

9/ Walter Lippmann
1021 Park Ave. at 85th St. (northeast corner).

He moved into this 17-room duplex apartment in 1966 and stayed until 1970. **Lippmann** had recently returned from Washington D.C. where he had lived for the last 30 years as political columnist for the *New York Times*.

10/ Steve Allen
1009 Park Ave. between 84th and 85th Street.

The first host of the television **Tonight Show** lived here in the late 1950's.

11/ P.G. Wodehouse
1000 Park Ave. at 84th St. (northwest corner).

The British comic novelist lived in a duplex apartment with a rooftop garden in this building with his third wife, Ethel, from 1948 until 1955. They had been forced to leave England after the Second World War when **Wodehouse** was accused of collaborating with the Germans. In the years while he lived in New York, he wrote a collection of short stories and four novels. In 1955, he moved to a small town on Long Island where he spent the rest of his life. He died in 1975.

12/ Eugene O'Neill
35 E. 84th St. at Madison Avenue.

O'Neill was 57 years old when he and his wife, **Carlotta**, rented a six-room penthouse apartment in this building in 1946. The playwright, then in failing health, had been living at Sea Island, Georgia for the last fourteen years. While he lived here, both *The Iceman Cometh* and *Moon for the Misbegotten* opened on the New York stage. The O'Neill's stayed here until the spring of 1948 when they moved to Boston.

13/ Harold Arlen
12 E. 86th St. near Fifth Avenue.

In the early 1930's, the composer of many popular songs lived in this apartment building, first on the main floor, then later in a tenth-floor penthouse. The place was then called the **Hotel Croydon**.

Ring Lardner also lived here briefly in the last years of his life.

14/ Otto Rank
2 E. 86th St. near Fifth Avenue.

The famed psychoanalyst lived in a three-room apartment here at the **Hotel Adams** in 1934-35, soon after moving to New York from Europe. **Rank** used the apartment as an office to see his patients. It was here that **Anais Nin** practiced as an analyst for a short period under Rank's tutelage.

15/ Bernard Baruch
1055 Fifth Ave. at 86th Street.

The Wall Street financier and presidential advisor bought a mansion on this site in the 1920's and lived here until 1946. Its six stories had 10 baths and 32 rooms, including an oval dining room, ballroom, smoking room lined with Norwegian pine, and a solarium. His wife of 41 years, **Annie Griffen**, died while they were living here in 1938. In 1946 Baruch moved to 4 E. 66th St. where he lived for the rest of this life (see Tour 3, Number 7 in this section). Number 1055 Fifth Ave. no longer exists; the mansion was demolished and replaced by this newer building numbered 1050.

16/ Oscar Hammerstein II
1067 Fifth Ave. between 87th and 88th Street.

The lyricist who collaborated with **Richard Rodgers** on so many Broadway musicals lived in this house, just south of the **Guggenheim**

Museum, in the 1930's. **Hammerstein** didn't team with Rodgers until they wrote *Oklahoma* together in 1943. He was a successful songwriter on his own long before then, gaining his greatest fame as the co-writer (with **Jerome Kern**) of *Show Boat* which opened in 1927.

17/ Sinclair Lewis
21 E. 90th St. at Madison Avenue.

The **Nobel Prize**-winning novelist lived in this apartment building with his second wife, journalist **Dorothy Thompson**, in 1931-32. While they lived here, they maintained two separate sitting rooms so that each could entertain their own guests without disturbing the other. Lewis and Thompson were divorced in 1942.

18/ Andrew Carnegie
2 E. 91st St. at Fifth Avenue.

The millionaire industrialist-philanthropist and founder of **U.S. Steel** built this 64-room mansion which was completed in 1901. The Georgian brick classical home was very technically advanced for its time with air conditioning, passenger elevators, and central heating. Carnegie's wife, **Louise**, continued to live here after his death in 1919. She died here in June 1946. It is now the **Cooper-Hewitt Museum** (Smithsonian Institution's National Museum of Design).

19/ Marjorie Merriweather Post and E.F. Hutton
1107 Fifth Ave. at 92nd Street.

The daughter of the founder of the **Post Cereal** empire and her famous stockbroker husband lived here from 1920 until their divorce in the mid-1930's. It was a mammoth 54 room, three-story apartment. Their only daughter, actress **Dina Merrill**, was raised here. The apartment has long since been subdivided.

Carnegie

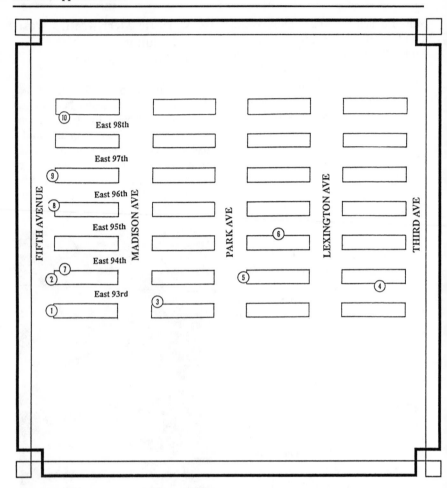

Tour 9

1/ John O'Hara
2/ Jacob Ruppert
3/ Billy Rose
4/ The Marx Brothers
5/ Moss Hart

6/ Mark Rothko
7/ George S. Kaufman
8/ Thomas Dewey
9/ Grantland Rice
10/ Clarence Day

Tour 9

1/ John O'Hara
1115 Fifth Ave. at 93rd Street.

O'Hara lived here in his mother-in-law's residence with his wife, **Belle**, after they returned from Europe in 1938. It was during this period that the author began writing the *"Pal Joey"* stories which were first published in the *New Yorker* and later were turned into a successful Broadway musical. (See Hotel Pierre in this section, Tour 1, Number 1.) Longtime *New York Times* publisher **Arthur Hays Sulzberger** also lived in this building for the last 16 years of his life. He died in 1968.

2/ Jacob Ruppert
1116 Fifth Ave. at 93rd St. (presently numbered 1120 Fifth Ave.).

Ruppert, millionaire owner of baseball's **Yankees** for over 40 years and the man who brought **Babe Ruth** to New York, lived in a large mansion this site for many years. (He was also the owner of the huge Ruppert Brewery at 1693 Third Ave. in Yorkville.) His mansion, which stood on the northeast corner of 93rd Street, was one of the first to be built in this part of Manhattan which was still made up of shanties and small farms at the turn of the century. The house and its large orchards in back were protected by an iron-spiked fence and two watchdogs.

The Marx Brothers, who lived only four blocks away when they were boys (see Number 4 below), regularly braved the fence and the dogs to pilfer the peaches and apples on Ruppert's trees.

3/ Billy Rose
56 E. 93rd St. at Madison Avenue.

The theatrical producer purchased this beautiful townhouse in 1956 from sportsman-businessman **William Goadby Loew**. Built in 1932, it was probably the last great mansion built in New York. It had 45 rooms. Rose lived here with his last two wives, divorcing both of them. He was living here when he died in 1965.

The mansion is now the **Smithers Alcoholism Center** of the St. Luke's-Roosevelt Hospital. Writer **John Cheever** was among those who received treatment here.

4/ The Marx Brothers
179 E. 93rd St. between Lexington and Third Avenue.

In 1895, **Sam** and **Minnie Marx** moved their family into a small flat in this four-story tenement building. There were 10 members in all.

In those days, this section of Yorkville was a poor Jewish neighborhood sandwiched between the Irish to the north and the Germans to the south. **Groucho** (Julius) was five years old at the time, **Harpo** (Adolf) was seven, **Chico** (Leonard) was eight. The Marxes lived here until 1910, when Minnie decided that the family vaudeville act, which she had organized a few years earlier, would fare better with Chicago as their home. They didn't return to New York permanently until the early 1920's. By then they were famous.

Marx Brothers: Harpo, Groucho & Chico

5/ Moss Hart
1185 Park Ave. between 93rd and 94th Street.

T his was the last New York home of the Broadway playwright and director. He was living here with his wife, **Kitty Carlisle**, when he directed the long-running Broadway musical, *My Fair Lady,* which opened in 1956. Hart moved to Palm Springs, California in 1961 just after selling this house. He died of a heart attack there a few weeks later.

6/ Mark Rothko
118 E. 95th St. between Park and Lexington Avenue.

R **othko** moved to this red brick building with his second wife, **Mell**, and his young daughter, Kate, in 1960. His son, Christopher, was born while they lived here in 1963. Rothko's studio was at 157 E. 69th St.; in January, 1969, he moved away from his family to live there (see this section, Tour 5, Number 5).

Marx Brothers Home
179 E. 93rd St.

7/ George S. Kaufman
14 E. 94th St. near Fifth Avenue.

The master Broadway playwright and director moved to this narrow, five-story house in 1932 with his wife, **Beatrice**.

He lived here during one of his most productive periods, writing and directing four hit plays including *You Can't Take It With You, George Washington Slept Here*, and *The Man Who Came to Dinner* (all co-written with **Moss Hart**) and *Stage Door* (co-written with **Edna Ferber**).

Kaufman lived here until 1943.

8/ Thomas E. Dewey
1148 Fifth Ave. at 96th Street.

Dewey was a 32-two-year-old district attorney when he moved into an eight-room apartment here with his wife and son in 1934.

He was living here in 1935 when he was appointed Special Prosecutor for New York City and proceeded to conduct the famous investigations of organized crime that led to the conviction of **Lucky Luciano** and many other underworld figures.

Dewey became New York governor in 1942 and lost the presidential elections of 1944 and 1948 as the Republican candidate.

9/ Grantland Rice
1158 Fifth Ave. at 97th Street.

This was the home of the famous sports writer for many years.

Rice gained fame while working for the *New York Tribune* in the 1920's and wrote a nationally syndicated column for 25 years.

He was living here in July 1954 when he died of a stroke. He was 73.

10/ Clarence Day
1170 Fifth Ave. at 98th Street.

The author, best known for his book, *Life with Father,* lived in this house from 1928 to 1934.

Day, badly crippled for most of his life, died of pneumonia in 1935--the year that his famous book was published.

It was made into a successful Broadway play in 1939.

Section Four:

The Upper West Side

The Ansonia

Home of Florenz Ziegfeld

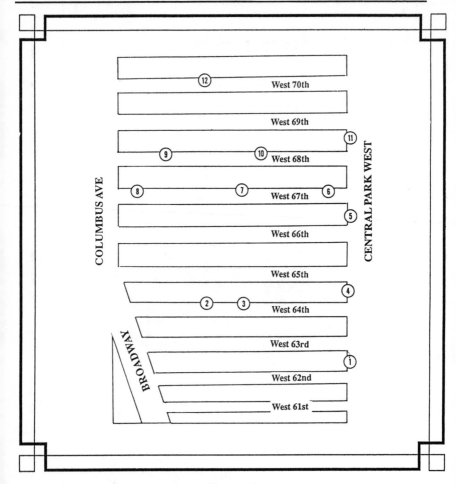

Tour 1

1/ Ethel Merman
2/ Legs Diamond
3/ Stewart and Fonda
4/ Edna Ferber
5/ Bob Hope
6/ Hotel des Artistes
7/ Robert Lowell
8/ Ben Hecht
9/ Dorothy Parker
10/ James Dean
11/ Rube Goldberg
12/ Bernard Baruch

The **Upper West Side** is defined for our purposes as the area between **Central Park West** and the **Hudson River**, and from **West 59th Street** to **West 106th Street**. Until the last years of the 19th century, this part of Manhattan consisted mainly of open spaces and scattered farmhouses and shanties. In 1884, the **Dakota**, New York's first luxury apartment house, opened along Central Park West, becoming this area's initial magnet for the middle class and the well-to-do. Intense development began to take place after 1900 when ethnic families, particularly Jews from Eastern Europe, began to move here from the Lower East Side as their fortunes improved.

Although the **Upper West Side** enjoyed a certain fashion with the very wealthy for a short period--at one time **Riverside Drive**, boasting a few large mansions, made an attempt to become a new *Millionaires' Row*--few of the private palaces similar to the ones seen along Fifth Avenue were built here and the area never achieved the opulence of the Upper East Side. A string of spectacular apartment houses along **Central Park West,** built between 1900 and 1930 near the Dakota, did give this side of the park an architectural distinction to match Fifth Avenue. But basically the West Side became a monument to middle class respectability. By the 1950's the Upper West Side had entered a period of decline, as its younger generation moved to other parts of Manhattan or escaped to the suburbs. But in recent years the neighborhood has made a dramatic comeback. It is the home of a number of artists, writers, and theater people. It continues to attract young professionals and their families who have discovered in the solid rows of substantial old houses excellent opportunities for restoration. One finds here today a great diversity of people, buildings, stores, and institutions. And, over the last century, it has been the home of many prominent New Yorkers.

Tour 1

1/ Ethel Merman
25 Central Park W. between 62nd and 63rd Street.

This large Art Deco building called the **Century Apartments** was erected in 1931 and **Merman** moved here in 1933. She was just becoming a Broadway star and during her residence here she appeared in such shows as *Anything Goes, Red, Hot and Blue!*, and *Panama Hattie*. Merman's apartment was on the 21st and 22nd floors and had a large roof terrace. Playwright **Marc** **Connelly** moved here in 1929 and made it his home for more than 40 years. **George Gershwin's** mother was living here at the Century when she died in 1948, almost 12 years after her famous son passed away.

2/ Jack "Legs" Diamond
35 W. 64th St. between Central Park West and Broadway.

The legendary gangster of the prohibition era kept a suite for his girlfriend, **Kiki Roberts**, in Room 824 of this building. Then called the **Hotel Monticello**, it was his New York headquarters in the late 1920's. In October, 1929, **Legs** and **Kiki**, dining in their pajamas here one night, were attacked by rival gunmen. Diamond was shot five times--and survived. Kiki was unharmed. It wasn't until 1931, in Albany, that his enemies succeeded in murdering Legs.

3/ James Stewart and Henry Fonda
25 W. 64th St. between Central Park West and Broadway.

In the fall of 1932, **Fonda**, recently divorced from his first wife, **Margaret Sullavan**, moved into a very small two-room apartment on the third floor of this old building. He shared it with his friend, **James Stewart**. They were joined by friends, **Josh Logan** and **Myron McCormick**. All four were young, struggling actors. The building was mainly a brothel in those days. They stayed here until 1933. Fonda and Stewart didn't break into the movies until 1935.

4/ Edna Ferber
50 Central Park W. at 65th St. (southwest corner).

This 1907 building known as the **Prasada** was **Ferber's** home from 1918 until the early 1920's. She moved here with her mother, **Julia**, after their arrival from Chicago. Ferber's novels were immediate popular successes. She won the **Pulitzer Prize** for *So Big* in 1924.

5/ Bob Hope
65 Central Park W. between 66th and 67th Street.

The comedian lived in this large apartment building in the 1930's with his wife, **Delores**. He was living here when he got his first big break in the musical, *Roberta*.

In 1936 he starred in **Cole Porter's** *Red, Hot and Blue!* with Ethel Merman, who lived only four blocks away from him (see number 1 above). Hope moved permanently to Hollywood in 1938.

6/ Hotel des Artistes
1 W. 67th St. off Central Park West.

This famous cooperative apartment building, opened in 1918, has been the home of many famous New Yorkers over the years.

Rudolph Valentino lived here with his second wife, **Natasha Rambova**, in 1922 and 1923. Writer **Fannie Hurst** owned a huge triplex here from 1932 until her death in 1968.

Alexander Woollcott lived here in the late 1920's.

Harry Crosby, the Paris expatriate and publisher of *Black Sun Press*, killed himself here in 1929.

Journalist **Heywood Broun** and his wife, **Ruth Hale**, moved here in 1933, just before they divorced.

Other residents have been **Noel Coward, Norman Rockwell, Isadora Duncan** and former New York Mayor **John V. Lindsay**.

Central Park Studios--Lowell's home

7/ Robert Lowell
15 W. 67th St. off Central Park West.

The poet lived here at the **Central Park Studios** during the 1960's. It was here in 1963 that the first issue of the *New York Review of Books* was created.

8/ Ben Hecht
39 W. 67th St. near Columbus Avenue.

Screenwriter and playwright **Hecht**, who co-authored *The Front Page* and *Twentieth Century*, lived in a 14th floor apartment here during the last years of his life. He died here in 1964.

9/ Dorothy Parker
57 W. 68th St. between Central Park West and Columbus Avenue.

The writer (her real name was **Dorothy Rothschild**) was six years old in 1899 when she moved into this five-story limestone row house with her family. Dorothy's mother had recently died and her father remarried soon after they moved here. Although she was Jewish, she attended a nearby Catholic convent school. The Rothschilds lived here until 1903.

10/ James Dean
19 W. 68th St. between Central Park West and Columbus Avenue.

The young actor had his first New York apartment here, on the top floor, in 1953. It was a small flat, very simply furnished, with one large porthole window. He was 22 years old at the time and was finding small roles on television and on the stage. **Dean** lived here until 1954 when he moved to California to perform in his first movie, *East of Eden.*

11/ Rube Goldberg, John Garfield
88 Central Park W. (southwest corner of 69th Street).

This 12-story brick and limestone building called the **Brentmore** was the home of the famous cartoonist for many years. **Goldberg**, best known for his creations of marvelously complicated contraptions designed to accomplish very simple ends, lived here until 1963. **John Garfield** made this

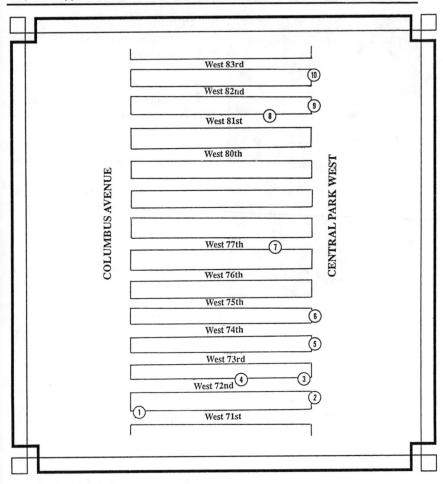

Tour 2

1/ William Sherman
2/ Majestic Apartments
3/ The Dakota
4/ Tennessee Williams
5/ Lee Strasberg
6/ Jack Dempsey
7/ Helen Morgan
8/ Mrs. Rudolph Valentino
9/ The Beresford
10/ Fanny Brice

building his last permanent home. He lived here in early 1952 with his wife and two children. He died in May of that year.

12/ Bernard Baruch
51 W. 70th St. between Central Park West and Columbus Avenue.

The **Wall Street** financier and presidential advisor grew to manhood in this five-story brownstone. His father was a prominent physician who had moved his family to New York from South Carolina in 1880 when Bernard was a boy. The young **Baruch** lived here until 1899 when, as a novice stockbroker, he made his first big killing on Wall Street.

Tour 2

1/ William Tecumseh Sherman
75 W. 71st St. at Columbus Avenue (northeast corner).

After he retired from the army, the Civil War general moved to New York and for the last four years of his life lived in a large house on this corner. He entertained here occasionally but frequently became a hermit, slipping away to a solitary basement office to read the novels of **Dickens** and the poetry of **Robert Burns**. In February, 1891, **Sherman** caught a severe cold while attending a wedding and within a few days died of pneumonia. He was 69.

2/ Majestic Apartments
115 Central Park W. at 72nd St. (southwest corner)

One of the most elegant and luxurious apartment houses in New York City, the twin-towered **Majestic Apartments** was built here on the site of the old **Hotel Majestic**, which was a prominent uptown resort from about 1893 to 1929.

The hotel was the onetime home of such notables as **Fred Astaire** and his sister, **Adele,** who lived here in 1919 and **George S. Kaufman** who moved in with his wife, **Beatrice**, after their marriage in 1917. Dancer **Isadora Duncan** lived here in 1915.

The *new* **Majestic Apartments**, opened in 1931, has been the residence of many famous and notorious persons. Underworld boss **Frank Costello** had a seven-room penthouse on the 18th floor for many years. A mob enemy shot and wounded him in the front lobby here on the night of May 2, 1957. Costello survived the attack and lived 16 more years. He died here of natural causes in 1973.

Costello's partners in crime, **Meyer Lansky** and **Lucky Luciano**, also lived here at one time.

Stage and movie director **Elia Kazan** lived in an apartment on the 16th floor here in the early 1960's. Journalist Walter Winchell and entertainers **Ted Lewis** and **Milton Berle** were also residents.

The Majestic became a cooperative in 1957.

3/ The Dakota
1 W. 72nd St. at Central Park West.

Built in 1884, the 10-story **Dakota** is the city's first luxury apartment house and one of the most famous residences in the world. It has been a prestige address, especially for those in the arts, since the 19th century when this part of New York City was so removed from the center of town that it was thought to be almost out in Dakota Territory.

Numerous notable people have lived here, including **Judy Holliday** (who died here in 1965), **Zachary Scott, Lauren Bacall** and **Jason Robards, Boris Karloff, Jose Ferrer** and **Rosemary Clooney**, and **Leonard Bernstein**.

The movie, *Rosemary's Baby*, was filmed here in 1968. Former Beatle **John Lennon** was murdered at the front entrance on December 8, 1980.

4/ Tennessee Williams
15 W. 72nd St. near Central Park West.

The playwright was 54 years old in 1965 when he moved into a large apartment on the 33rd floor of this building which stands next to the **Dakota.** It was a low point in **Williams'** life. He became dependent on various drugs and was extremely depressed much of the time. In 1968 he moved away from here to live in a series of residences. He recovered his health in 1969 after undergoing drug treatment in St. Louis.

5/ Lee Strasberg
135 Central Park W. between 73rd and 74th Street.

This famous luxury apartment known as the **Langham** was the home of the famous drama teacher for many years. **Strasberg** moved here in the 1950's with his wife, **Paula Miller**, and was living here in 1982 when he died of a heart attack. Actor **Basil Rathbone** also made the Langham his home at one time.

6/ Jack Dempsey
145-146 Central Park W. between 74th and 75th Street.

This huge, twin-towered cooperative building is the **San Remo** and it has been the residence of many notable New Yorkers, past and present. **Dempsey** had a 14-room apartment here for a number of years after his boxing career was over. More recently, it was the home of the songwriter **Harold Arlen** who died here in April, 1986, at the age of 81. Actress **Rita Hayworth** lived here during her last years until her death in 1987.

7/ Helen Morgan
6 W. 77th St. near Central Park West.

The legendary nightclub and Broadway singer was 19 when she lived in a small apartment here, across from the **American Museum of Natural History** in 1919.

She had recently moved to New York from Chicago with her mother, **Lulu**. Her first job came soon after, in the chorus line of a **Ziegfeld** production.

Morgan became famous in 1927 when she starred in the Broadway musical, *Show Boat.*

8/ Mrs. Rudolph Valentino
9 W. 81st St. near Central Park West.

Valentino's second wife, **Natasha Rambova**, lived here in 1925 during the period of their separation and divorce. Valentino was at the height of his popularity at the time. He died suddenly in New York in 1926.

9/ The Beresford
211 Central Park W. at 81st Street (northwest corner).

This huge apartment house, built in 1929, is one of the most famous residences in New York.

Poet **Sara Teasdale** moved here in 1917 with her husband, **Ernst Felsinger**. Their apartment on the third floor was her New York home for the next 10 years.

Underworld boss **Meyer Lansky** lived here from 1943 until 1948. He was divorced from his first wife, **Anna**, during that period.

Anthropologist **Margaret Mead** made the **Beresford** her home from 1966 until her death in 1978. Her office at the **American Museum of Natural History** was only four blocks away.

Actor **Rock Hudson** made this his New York home until his death in 1985.

10/ Fanny Brice, Sara Teasdale
230 Central Park W. at 83rd Street (southwest corner).

Brice and **Teasdale** lived here at the **Bolivar Apartments** at different times. Brice, then a major star of the **Ziegfeld Follies**, rented a 10-room apartment here with her husband, gambler **Nicky Arnstein**, in 1918, soon after their marriage. They stayed until 1921.

The poet **Teasdale** moved here in 1930 soon after her divorce from her husband, **Ernst**. She stayed until 1932. She died a year later.

Tour 3

1/ Bix Beiderbecke
119 W. 71st St. between Columbus and Broadway.

The legendary jazz cornetist was 21 years old in 1924 when he came to New York for the first time with a band called the **Wolverines**. He lived in this building during his stay. **Beiderbecke** left the Wolverines soon after his arrival and played with other groups. When he came back to New York in 1926 with the **Jean Godkette Orchestra** to play at **Roseland**, he gained instant stardom.

2/ Mark Rothko
137 W. 72nd St. between Columbus and Amsterdam Avenue.

The artist was 29 years old when he married his first wife, **Edith Sachar**, in 1932. They took an apartment in this building with the twin towers soon after the wedding.

In addition to his painting, **Rothko** worked as a part-time teacher at the **Brooklyn Jewish Center**. It was a job he retained for many years until he became financially successful as an artist. Edith designed costume jewelry. They lived here until 1936.

3/ The Ansonia
2107 Broadway between West 73rd and 74th Street.

This is a landmark on the Upper West Side and one of New York's most famous apartment buildings. The ornate **Ansonia**, with its Beaux-Arts style decoration, gargoyles, rounded-corner towers, and iron balconies, has been the home of many prominent people since it opened in 1904.

Because its thick walls are virtually soundproof, it has always attracted musical artists who could practice without disturbing their neighbors. Among the notable ones who have lived here are **Enrico Caruso, Arturo Toscanini, Igor Stravinsky, Yehudi Menuhin, Lily Pons, Ezio Pinza,** and **Feodor Chaliapin.**

Showman **Florenz Ziegfeld** made the Ansonia his residence for many years. At one time he occupied a 13-room suite on the 10th floor with his Follies star, wife **Anna Held**, while at the same time maintaining an exact duplicate suite on the 13th floor for his mistress, **Lillian Lorraine**.

Later, Ziegfeld lived here with his wife, actress **Billie Burke.**

Ziegfield

Members of the infamous **Chicago White Sox** team of 1919 were staying here at the Ansonia when they conspired to fix the World Series that year. They came to be known as the Black Sox when their actions were exposed.

Babe Ruth moved here in 1920 when he joined the **New York Yankees** and stayed until his second marriage in 1929.

Novelist **Theodore Dreiser** lived alone in a two-room suite on the 14th floor from 1931 until 1935.

At one time, the basement of the Ansonia housed the infamous **Continental Baths**, where singer **Bette Midler** first gained prominence in the 1960's.

4/ Anais Nin
158 W. 75th St. between Columbus and Amsterdam Avenue.

The writer was 14 when she moved into this white brick and stone

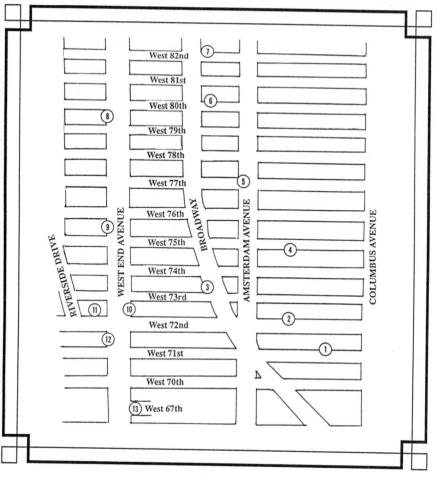

Tour 3

1/ Bix Beiderbecke
2/ Mark Rothko
3/ Hotel Ansonia
4/ Anais Nin
5/ Polly Adler
6/ Anais Nin
7/ J.D. Salinger

8/ Meyer Lansky
9/ Charles Evans Hughes
10/ Marlon Brando
11/ Charles Schwab
12/ Sara Teasdale
13/ Duke Ellington

house with her mother and brothers in May, 1917. She left school in the following year to support her family by working as a fashion mannequin and artists' model. Nin stayed here until she left New York at the end of 1919. She lived in Europe during the 1920's and didn't return to New York until 1934.

5/ Polly Adler
77th Street and Amsterdam Avenue.

In the early 1930's, New York's most famous "madam" maintained a bordello in an apartment house on this corner, probably in the brown brick building at 201 W. 77th St.

6/ Anais Nin
219 W. 80th St. between Broadway and Amsterdam Avenue.

In 1914, at the age of 11, after her father had deserted the family, **Nin** moved from Barcelona to New York with her mother and brothers. In November, 1915, they moved into "a pretty little apartment on the third floor" of this old building. They stayed until May, 1917, when they moved to a house on West 75th Street (see number 4 above). This building has recently been renovated.

7/ J.D. Salinger
221 W. 82nd St. at Broadway.

The author of *Catcher in the Rye* lived as a boy from 1928 to 1932 in Apartment 10G of this 14-story brick building. His father was in the ham and cheese importing business. By the time **Salinger** was 13, the family was af-

fluent enough to move to a Park Avenue apartment on the Upper East Side (See Section Three, Tour 8, Number 3).

8/ Meyer Lansky
411 West End Ave. between 79th and 80th Street.

The underworld boss moved to an apartment here in the late 1930's with his first wife, **Anna**. After **Lansky** and his partner **Lucky Luciano** had arranged the murder of rival **Dutch Schultz** in 1935, they became the dominant leaders of organized crime in New York. Four decades later, Lansky would stand alone as the undisputed leader of the mob--the *Chairman of the Board,* as he was known, of the **National Crime Syndicate.** He lived here at 411 West End until 1943.

9/ Charles Evans Hughes
329 West End Ave. at 75th Street (northwest corner).

Hughes moved to a house on this site in 1893 while he was a young attorney. He stayed until 1905. Hughes was elected New York governor a year later as the Republican candidate, defeating Democrat **William Randolph Hearst.** The address of this building has been renumbered. There is a memorial plaque on the wall of the house at 75th Street.

10/ Marlon Brando
270 West End Ave. at 73rd Street.

This apartment building with the gray awning in front was the place where **Brando's** mother, **Dorothy Pen-**

nebaker **Brando**, lived in the mid-1940's. Marlon lived here with her and his two sisters, **Frances and Jocelyn**, in an 11th-floor corner apartment beginning in 1944. He was then a young actor appearing on Broadway in the play, *I Remember Mama*. Brando lived here off and on over the next few years.

Mae West also lived in this same block at 266 West End Ave.

11/ Charles M. Schwab
72nd Street and Riverside Drive (northwest corner).

Schwab, the industrialist and financier, built and moved into a massive four-story red brick Georgian mansion on this corner in 1906. It was one of the most prominent landmarks on the Upper West Side until it was demolished in 1948.

12/ Sara Teasdale
243 West End Ave. at 71st Street.

The poet moved to a furnished apartment here in the fall of 1929 just after her divorce from **Ernst Filsinger**. This building was known as the **Hotel Cardinal** in those days. **Teasdale** moved away in the summer of the following year.

13/ Duke Ellington
140 West End Ave. between 66th and 67th Streets.

Ellington's last New York residence was an apartment on the 22nd floor of this huge, modern apartment complex called the **Lincoln Towers**. He shared it with **Evie Ellis**, his companion for many years. He was living here when he died on May 24, 1974.

Tour 4

1/ George Gershwin
33 Riverside Drive at 75th Street.

Gershwin lived in this large apartment building from 1929 until 1933. It was a large bachelor penthouse on the 17th floor overlooking the Hudson River. His brother, **Ira**, lived next door. The two apartments had the feverish atmosphere of a railroad station with people coming and going, sometimes for business, sometimes socially, and with parties continuing into the early morning hours as Gershwin played his piano and sang for his guests. While he lived here, he finished *Porgy and Bess* and also wrote the music for such shows as *Girl Crazy* and *Of Thee I Sing*.

2/ Fanny Brice
306 W. 76th St. between Riverside Drive and West End Avenue.

The musical comedy star bought this five-story, 20-room townhouse from the Colgate Soap family in the early 1920's and lived here with husband, **Nicky Arnstein**, until their divorce in 1927. She took the lower three floors for herself and rented the top two floors to theatrical friends. **Brice** was a legendary hostess. Her home was the scene of many lively parties that began after her nightly **Zieg-**

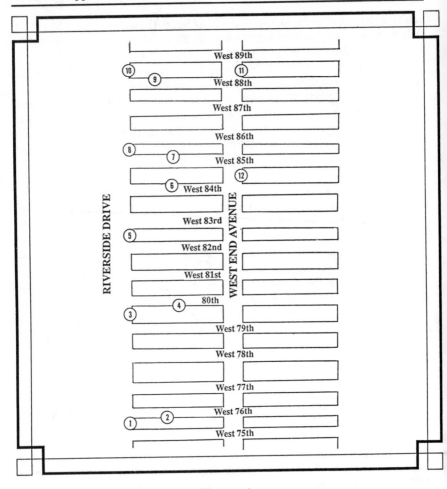

Tour 4

1/ George Gershwin
2/ Fanny Brice
3/ Marc Chagall
4/ Dorothy Parker
5/ Babe Ruth
6/ Arnold Rothstein
7/ Heywood Broun
8/ William Randolph Hearst
9/ Babe Ruth
10/ Brooks Atkinson
11/ Waxey Gordon
12/ Theda Bara

feld Follies performance and continued until she could no longer keep her guests awake.

3/ Marc Chagall
75 Riverside Drive between 79th and 80th Street.

In late 1944, still in grief over the recent death of his wife, the painter moved into a large double apartment in this towered house with his daughter, **Ida**, and her husband.

The studio where **Chagall** worked here had a beautiful view of the Hudson River. While living here, he met his future second wife, **Virginia**, who was then married to someone else. They moved together to a house in upstate New York in 1945. Chagall moved back to France in 1948.

4/ Dorothy Parker
310 W. 80th St. between Riverside Drive and West End Avenue.

The writer was 20 years old in 1913 when she was living here with her widower father, **Henry Rothschild**. He was a retired businessman who had worked in the wholesale garment trade.

Dorothy had attended the **Blessed Sacrament Convent**, a block away on 79th Street until 1907 and then spent a year at a girls boarding school in New Jersey before dropping out at age 14. When her father died here at the end of 1913, Dorothy moved away and began her career as a writer.

5/ Babe Ruth
110 Riverside Drive at 83rd Street (entrance on 83rd Street).

This was **Ruth's** last residence. He had been retired from baseball for seven years when he rented an 11-room apartment in this building with his second wife, **Claire Hodgson**, in 1942. He was living here when he died of throat cancer in August, 1948, at the age of 53.

6/ Arnold Rothstein
355 W. 84th St. between Riverside Drive and West End Avenue.

Rothstein was a notorious New York gambler who became a chief financier and mastermind of organized crime in the 1920's. He lived in this beautiful, three-story stone and brick house for a number of years with his wife, **Carolyn**. He was living here in 1919 when he was identified as the alleged fixer of the **World Series** between Chicago's "Black Sox" and the Cincinnati Reds. Rothstein was never prosecuted for the fix. He was murdered by an unidentified assailant in 1928 (See Section One, Tour 3, Number 20).

7/ Heywood Broun
333 W. 85th St. between Riverside Drive and West End Avenue.

Broun, one of the most prominent American journalists of our time, lived in this four-story brownstone with his wife, **Ruth Hale**, and their three-year old son, **Heywood Hale Broun**, from 1921 to 1928. In their first year here, they shared it with *New Yorker* editor **Harold Ross** and his wife, **Jane Grant.**

8/ William Randolph Hearst
137 Riverside Drive at 86th Street (entrance on 86th Street).

In 1908, the multi-millionaire newspaper tycoon rented a huge apartment on the top three floors of this building called the **Clarendon.**

By then, he needed a much larger residence for his family of three and an ever-growing collection of art objects that was expanding to museum size. This apartment had 30 rooms--it was one of the largest in Manhattan.

By 1913, the three floors were inadequate for his continually growing collection so **Hearst** bought the building for about $2 million and tore down the eighth and ninth floors to make a vast three-story room fronting on the Hudson River with walls some 35 feet high. When he finished these alterations, he probably had the biggest apartment in the world.

Hearst made this his New York home for many years. By the 1930's, he was spending most of his time with his mistress, **Marion Davies,** but his wife continued to live here until 1938 when Hearst, in financial trouble, was forced to sell the building.

Bara

building in April, 1929, after their wedding. The next day, Ruth hit a home run for his new bride in the first game of the season. Ruth retired from baseball in 1935. He lived in this building until 1942.

9/ Babe Ruth
345 W. 88th St. between Riverside Drive and West End Avenue.

Ruth, with his second wife, **Claire Hodgson,** moved into an 11-room apartment on the seventh floor of this

10/ Brooks Atkinson
160 Riverside Drive between 88th and 89th Street.

This was the home of the man who was the *New York Times* theater critic from 1925 until 1960. **Atkinson's** influence on the success or failure of Broadway productions was so great that he was referred to as the *"autocrat of the aisle seat."*

11/ Waxey Gordon
590 West End Ave. between 88th and 89th Street.

Irving Wexler, alias *"Waxey Gordon,"* was a notorious mobster and racketeer who became the multimillionaire king of bootlegging in Harlem and the West Side in the 1920's and early 1930's. His luxuriously furnished 10-room apartment here, complete with six domestic servants, was said to have a handsome library with $4,200 worth of unopened books. Gordon's career ended in 1933 when the famous crime commission headed by prosecutor **Thomas Dewey** sent him to prison for 10 years.

12/ Theda Bara
500 West End Ave. at 84th Street.

The silent-screen actress known as *"the Vamp"* lived in this large apartment building in the early 1920's as her movie career was fading.

Tour 5

1/ Jerome Kern
206 W. 92nd St. between Broadway and Amsterdam Avenue.

The man who composed a long list of memorable popular songs including the music for the Broadway hit, *Show Boat*, took an apartment in this brownstone in 1913 with his wife, **Eva. Kern** was 28 years old and busy writing songs for various New York shows. They stayed here until 1916 when they purchased a house in Bronxville, New York, where they lived for many years.

2/ St. Gregory's Catholic Church
144 W. 90th St. between Amsterdam and Columbus Avenue.

It was here on April 17, 1929, that **Babe Ruth** married his second wife, **Claire Hodgson.** Their new home was only a few blocks away at 345 W. 88th St. (see Tour 4, Number 9, this section).

3/ Richard Rodgers
161 W. 86th St. between Amsterdam and Columbus Avenue.

The Broadway composer was nine years old when he and his family moved into this brick apartment building in 1911. His future musical partner, **Oscar Hammerstein II**, then 16 years old, lived only two blocks away at 87th Street and Central Park West, although they didn't meet until years later. **Rodgers** remained here with his parents until he was 27. He moved out in 1929, not long before he married his life-long spouse, **Dorothy Feiner.** Rodgers was living here in 1919 when he first met **Lorenz Hart** and formed the legendary musical partnership that lasted nearly 25 years.

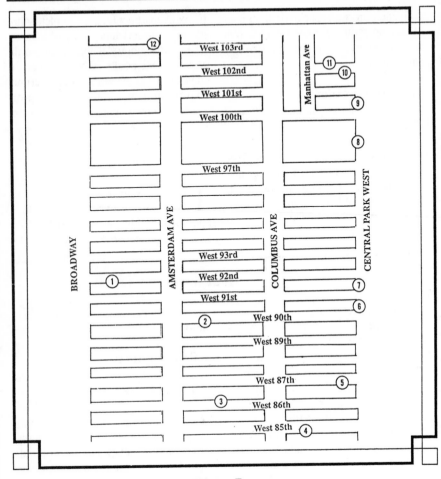

Tour 5

1/ Jerome Kern
2/ St. Gregory's Church
3/ Richard Rodgers
4/ John McGraw
5/ Billie Holiday
6/ Sinclair Lewis

7/ Lorenz Hart
8/ Herman Mankiewicz
9/ Duke Ellington
10/ Theodore Dreiser
11/ Mark Rothko
12/ John Coltrane

4/ John McGraw and Christy Mathewson
76 W. 85th St. near Columbus Avenue.

McGraw, one of baseball's greatest managers, who led the **New York Giants** to 10 National League pennants and three world championships between 1902 and 1932, rented a seven-room apartment in this building with his wife, beginning in 1903.

Living with them was McGraw's star pitcher of those years, **Christy Mathewson** and his wife. They paid $50 a month. The elevated train that ran uptown to the **Polo Grounds**, where they played, was only a block away. The Mathewsons paid for the food and the McGraws settled the rent and gas bill. McGraw led the Giants to league championships in 1903 and 1904 and Mathewson was baseball's best pitcher in those years, winning 30 and 33 games respectively.

5/ Billie Holiday
26 W. 87th St. near Central Park West.

The legendary blues singer lived in a small one-and-a-half room apartment here during the last two years of her life. During that period, she was too ill to work regularly; short of money, she spent much of her time here alone. She collapsed in her apartment on May 31, 1959, and was rushed to **Metropolitan Hospital** in Harlem where she died of heart failure on July 17. She was 44.

6/ Sinclair Lewis
300 Central Park W. between 90th and 91st Street.

In January, 1943, **Lewis** rented a large duplex penthouse here at this twin-towered Art Deco building called the **Eldorado**. He had recently divorced his second wife, journalist **Dorothy Thompson**. This was the last New York home of the **Nobel Prize**-winning novelist. He became increasingly unhappy living in Manhattan and finally, in April, 1945, he moved to Duluth, Minnesota. Lewis died in Rome in 1951.

7/ Lorenz Hart
320 Central Park W. at 92nd Street (southwest corner).

The lyricist who teamed with **Richard Rodgers** to write a long string of Broadway musicals rented a large duplex apartment here at the **Ardsley** during the last decade of his life. **Hart,** a life-long bachelor, lived here with his mother and father.

He entertained constantly. Friends were amazed that he got any songwriting done at all because he was usually up all night; the parties would start from scratch at midnight with anyone and everyone invited. Hart moved to the **Hotel Delmonico** in 1943, the year of his death. (See Section Two, Tour 1, Number 5).

8/ Herman Mankiewicz
378 Central Park W. between West 97th and 100th Street.

Mankiewicz was a journalist, drama critic, movie producer, screenwriter, and one of the wittiest members of the **Algonquin Group**. He is probably best remembered as the co-writer of the **Orson Welles** film, *Citizen Kane*. From 1923 to 1926, Mankiewicz lived in an apartment on this site, now taken over by the huge **Park West Village** apartment complex. During that period he was a drama critic for the *New York Times* and the *New Yorker.* He moved to Hollywood permanently in 1926.

9/ Duke Ellington
400 Central Park W. between 100th and 101st Street.

Ellington lived here for a number of years in the 1950's. He was still legally married to his first wife but they had separated many years before and Ellington shared this apartment with **Evie Ellis**, the woman he lived with until his death in 1974.

10/ Theodore Dreiser
6 W. 102nd St. near Central Park West.

In 1899 **Dreiser** was a young writer, newly married, when he moved into an apartment in this brownstone building. It was here that he wrote his famous first novel, *Sister Carrie.* This was a comfortable middle-class neighborhood in those days and, at $35 a month, the flat was an expensive one for a freelance writer with little money. Number 6 has since been merged with the adjacent buildings. The entrance is now in the back of the building.

11/ Mark Rothko
19 W. 102nd St. between Central Park West and Manhattan Avenue.

Dreiser

Rothko rented a room in a building on this site, now an empty lot, in the 1920's. He moved here in 1924 soon after arriving in New York from Yale University. During that period Rothko became an artist by chance when he wandered into an art class to meet a friend who was taking the course. Soon after, he began to study at the **Art Students League** while supporting himself with odd jobs. He lived here until 1929.

12/ John Coltrane
203 W. 103rd St. at Amsterdam Avenue.

Coltrane, the great jazz musician who revolutionized the saxophone, lived in a small, sparsely-furnished apartment on the second floor of this building from 1957 to 1959. He had just made the move to New York from Philadelphia with his wife, **Naida**, and his young stepdaughter. For a considerable time, all three slept on one mattress. He spent most of his day here lifting weights and practicing his horn. It was during this period that he played with the **Miles Davis Sextet**.

Tour 6

1/ John Dos Passos
214 Riverside Drive at 93rd Street.

Dos Passos rented an apartment here in 1932 while he worked on *The Big Money* which was the third volume of his trilogy, *U.S.A.* He was 36 years old.

2/ Lillian Hellman
330 W. 95th St. between West End Avenue and Riverside Drive.

This was **Hellman's** New York childhood home. In 1911 she was six years old when she moved with her family to an apartment on the 10th floor of this building. Her father, **Max**, had become a traveling salesman and the Hellmans split their time between New York and New Orleans, where Lillian was born. She lived in this house until 1925 when she married dramatist **Arthur Kober**.

3/ Pomander Walk
94th to 95th Streets, between Broadway and West End Avenue (261-267 W. 94th St. and 260-266 W. 95th St.)

This double row of small Tudor-style townhouses was inspired by a play of the same name that arrived on Broadway from London in 1911. The houses were modeled after the stage sets used for the New York production. They were built in 1921 and were originally intended for tenants in the acting profession. **Madeleine Carroll, Rosalind Russell, Louis Wolheim, Humphrey Bogart**, and **Lillian** and **Dorothy Gish** are among those who have lived here.

4/ Damon Runyon
251 W. 95th St. at Broadway.

The famed journalist and author of *Guys and Dolls* lived here for a period in the mid-1920's with his first wife, **Ellen**. He was **William Randolph Hearst's** top writer for the *New York Journal* at that time. The **Runyons'** apartment was on the top floor overlooking 96th and Broadway. The neighborhood was very colorful in those days; it was one of the favorite haunts of bootleggers and gangsters of the period.

5/ Spencer Tracy and Pat O'Brien
790 West End Avenue between 98th and 99th Street.

Tracy was a young actor attending classes at the **American Academy of Dramatic Arts** in 1922 when he rented a room in this building (now numbered 788) with fellow student, **Pat O'Brien**. The room was drab, sparsely furnished, and was only 12 by 12 in size with two iron bedsteads taking up nearly all the space. Usually short of money, they subsisted on pretzels, rice, and water. Since their clothing measurements were almost identical, Tracy and O'Brien were able to collect one wardrobe which they shared.

By the early 1930's, both actors had graduated from small theater roles to the movies. O'Brien is probably best

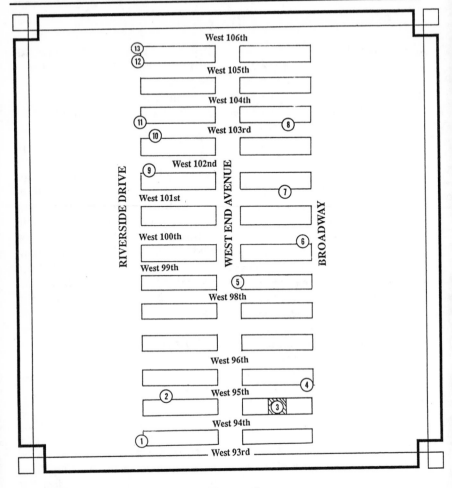

Tour 6

1/ John Dos Passos
2/ Lillian Hellman
3/ Pomander Walk
4/ Damon Runyon
5/ Spencer Tracy
6/ George Gershwin
7/ George S. Kaufman
8/ Humphrey Bogart
9/ Damon Runyon
10/ George Gershwin
11/ Otto Rank
12/ Marion Davies
13/ Saul Bellow

remembered for his movie role as *Knute Rockne of Notre Dame.*

6/ George Gershwin

250 W. 100th St. between Broadway and West End Avenue.

Gershwin rented a suite here at the Whitehall Hotel in the 1920's during the period when he lived with his family in the house at 316 W. 103rd St. (see number 10 below). He moved here for short periods when he had immediate writing deadlines to meet and the house was too noisy. It was here in 1928 that he started to compose *An American in Paris.*

7/ George S. Kaufman

241 W. 101st St. between Broadway and West End Avenue.

Kaufman was 21 in 1913 when he returned to New York from a brief stay in Washington D.C. and moved into his parents' nine-room apartment here. He soon found work as a reporter for the *New York Tribune* and in 1915 he became a columnist for the *New York Evening Mail.* Kaufman lived here until his marriage to **Beatrice Bakrow** in 1917. By the early 1920's, in collaboration with **Marc Connelly**, Kaufman began to achieve his first successes as a Broadway playwright.

8/ Humphrey Bogart

245 W. 103rd St. between Broadway and West End Avenue.

This four-story house was the actor's first residence. **Bogart**, born in 1900, was the son of a prominent physician, **Dr. Belmont DeForest Bogart.** His mother, **Maude**, was a well-known magazine illustrator. This neighborhood was very fashionable at the turn of the century--across the street stood the **Hotel Marseilles**, a residential hotel where **Sara Delano Roosevelt**, FDR's mother, lived for a number of years. The Bogarts had one of the few houses on the block with a telephone.

At age 13, Humphrey enrolled at **Trinity School** at 147 W. 91st St. near Amsterdam Avenue. He was a precocious child.

In 1917 he was sent to the exclusive **Phillips Academy** in Andover, Massachusetts, where he was soon asked to leave for infraction of the rules and "excessive high spirits." Bogart enlisted in the U.S. Navy in 1918 but returned to his third-floor room here in 1919 after his discharge.

By the early 1920's he was beginning to perform in small roles on the New York stage.

9/ Damon Runyon

320 W. 102nd St. near Riverside Drive.

In the early 1920's **Runyon**, with his first wife, **Ellen**, lived in a seven-room apartment here, overlooking the Hudson River.

Although it was his official address, he was gone most of the time, preferring to spend his days and nights with the people in the hotels, bars, restaurants, and theaters along Broadway that he made famous in his newspaper columns and short stories.

10/ George and Ira Gershwin
316 W. 103rd St. between Riverside Drive and West End Avenue.

The entire **Gershwin** family (including parents **Rose** and **Morris**, daughter **Judy**, and sons **Arthur, George**, and **Ira**) lived in this five-story white granite house from 1925 to 1931. It was a popular meeting place and general hangout for all of their friends and colleagues.

When **Ira** married **Lee Strunsky** in 1926, they took over the fourth floor. The fifth floor was **George's** sanctum. Here, in spite of the constant noise and distraction, he did his composing. When conditions became too frantic, he moved for a few days at a time to the **Whitehall Hotel** (see number 6 above).

George and Ira created much of their best-known music while they lived here. The plaque in front of the house commemorates those years.

11/ Otto Rank
310 Riverside Drive at 103rd Street.

The famous psychoanalyst moved to this apartment building called the **Hotel Master** in 1935 and lived here until the end of his life. Three months before his death, he married his long-time companion, **Estelle Buel**. He was 55 when he died in October, 1939.

12/ Marion Davies
331 Riverside Drive between 105th and 106th Street.

The musical comedy star met the millionaire newspaper publisher **William Randolph Hearst** in 1917 while she was performing in the **Ziegfeld Follies**. She was his life-long companion until his death in 1951. Her entire family benefited from the relationship. In 1918, Miss Davies moved with them to this white marble townhouse. Hearst spent more than $1 million redecorating it for her. At the same time, he established **Cosmopolitan Studios** to produce her films. She soon became a popular film comedy actress. Later he moved her and her entire family to California.

13/ Saul Bellow, Duke Ellington
333 Riverside Drive between 105th and 106th Street.

The **Nobel Prize**-winning novelist lived in this white brick house in the mid-1950's. He was staying here when he wrote *Seize the Day*.

This was officially **Duke Ellington's** sister **Ruth's** apartment, but from 1961 until his death in 1974, the jazz composer and bandleader stayed here frequently when he was in New York. (He also lived at 140 West End Ave. during the same period. See this section, tour 3, number 13.)

Section Five:

Chelsea and Surroundings

450 West 23rd Street

Home of Edwin Arlington Robinson

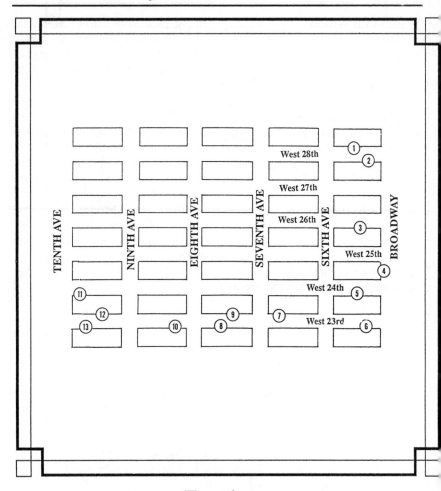

Tour 1

1/ George Gershwin
2/ Zero Mostel
3/ O. Henry
4/ William Randolph Hearst
5/ Stanford White
6/ Edith Wharton
7/ Stephen Crane

8/ Chelsea Hotel
9/ William Saroyan
10/ Mad Dog Coll
11/ John O'Hara
12/ Clement Clarke Moore
13/ Edwin Arlington Robinson

The Chelsea section of New York, which stretches from West 14th Street to West 30th Street and between Broadway and the Hudson River, has been an area of ups and downs in its 200-year history. Never exclusively a wealthy place nor one of extreme poverty, it is instead a diverse patchwork of ethnic groups living and working in a neighborhood of fine row houses, churches, tenements, factories, and housing projects.

Chelsea began as a private estate in 1750 and was named by its owner after the Chelsea Hospital in London. It was developed as a residential neighborhood in 1830 by Clement Moore, who is better known as the author of the Christmas poem, "A Visit from St. Nicholas." Chelsea's ethnic diversity started with the Irish who came in the 1830's to work in the factories along the Hudson River. In the 1880's, the city's first theater district was located here before it moved uptown. In the late 19th century, Chelsea was New York's bohemian district for artists and writers before Greenwich Village took over that role. It was also an early center for the motion picture industry before California lured it away.

Today Chelsea is one of Manhattan's most colorful neighborhoods. It continues to be the home of a wide range of ethnic groups. Although it is still a working class neighborhood, many young professionals have moved here recently to live in the newly renovated rowhouses. Also in the last few years, a number of people in the creative arts have again moved here from Greenwich Village and elsewhere. They continue an important tradition because Chelsea has been home to many famous New York writers, artists, musicians, and actors of the last century.

Tour 1

1/ George Gershwin
45 W. 28th St. between Broadway and Sixth Avenue.

In 1914, this block--West 28th Street between Fifth and Sixth Avenues-- was the heart of the old **Tin Pan Alley**, the center of America's music publishing business. In that year, **Gershwin**, then only 15 years old, took his first job as a piano-playing song demonstrator for the **Jerome H. Remick Music Company** in this old four-story building. While he worked here, he began to experiment with his own compositions. Two of his customers were **Fred** and

Gershwin

Adele Astaire, then a teenage song-and-dance team in vaudeville who later starred in two Gershwin Broadway musicals. The young Gershwin worked here at Remick's until 1917 when he left to write and publish his own songs.

2/ Zero Mostel
42 W. 28th St. between Broadway and Sixth Avenue.

The actor (and painter) had an apartment and studio here during the last years of his life.

3/ O. Henry
28 W. 26th St. between Broadway and Sixth Avenue.

This old seven-story building with the front fire escapes was known as the **Hotel Caledonia** when **William S. Porter**, better known as **O. Henry**, resided here. It was his last home.

The writer, then in failing health, moved here in 1906. In November, 1907, he married **Sara Coleman** in North Carolina and they moved into the **Chelsea Hotel**, just a few blocks away. But O. Henry retained his room here at the Caledonia for writing purposes.

He collapsed here on June 3, 1910, and died two days later in the hospital. He was 45 years old.

4/ William Randolph Hearst
1865 Broadway between 24th and 25th Street.

Hearst was a successful newspaperman from San Francisco when he moved to New York in 1895 to take over the *New York Journal*. He moved into a bachelor apartment on this site (the building here today is numbered 1123 Broadway). It adjoined the **Hoffman House,** which was one of Manhattan's most celebrated hotels of that era.

In 1897, Hearst moved across the street to the **Worth House**, a small but fashionable apartment building standing on the northwest corner of 25th Street across from **Worth Square.** He lived there until 1900.

It was during this period that Hearst engaged **Joseph Pulitzer** and his *New York World* in an infamous newspaper circulation war.

5/ Stanford White
22 W. 24th St. between Broadway and Sixth Avenue.

This old, dilapidated five-story building is the location of the famous architect's studio loft where in 1901 he supposedly began a well-publicized affair with a young showgirl named **Evelyn Nesbit**.

She became known as *"The Girl on the Red Velvet Swing."* (The swing hung from the ceiling of **White's** loft here.) Five years later, on June 25, 1906, Nesbit's husband, millionaire **Harry Thaw**, in a jealous rage, shot and killed White on the roof garden of the old **Madison Square Garden**.

In one of the most sensational criminal trials of the century, Thaw was acquitted on the grounds of insanity.

Wharton

6/ Edith Wharton
14 W. 23rd St. between Broadway and Sixth Avenue.

In 1862, the novelist was born in a brownstone on this site (probably the building, with altered facade, that stands here today). When she was four, the family moved to Europe for six years but they returned in 1872 and Edith lived on this street until her marriage in 1885. The address is half a block away from the **Flatiron Building**. **Wharton's** home was a rather cheerless place. The overcrowded rooms, like those of most New York townhouses of that era were so designed as to lack any clear identity and to make privacy difficult. Edith's first memory was of walking along Fifth Avenue in 1865 with her father, past brownstone houses and a fenced-in yard where a cow was pastured.

7/ Stephen Crane
165 W. 23rd St. between Sixth and Seventh Avenue.

The author of *The Red Badge of Courage* was a down-and-out 24-year-old journalist when he moved into a large room at the top of this five-story red building. The year was 1896. He spent his time writing newspaper and magazine articles about vice and poverty in the city along with an occasional short story. An observer described the huge, sparely furnished room as curiously typical of **Crane**: "An ink-bottle, a pen and a pad of paper occupy dots in the vast green expense. A sofa stretches itself near the window and tries to fill space. No crowded comfort is here--no luxury of ornament--no literature, classic or periodical: nothing but the man and his mind."

8/ Chelsea Hotel
222 W. 23rd St. between Seventh and Eighth Avenue.

The elegantly shabby **Chelsea Hotel**, with its well-won reputation as a mecca for artists and eccentrics, is a New York cultural and architectural landmark. It was opened in 1884 as a cooperative apartment house but when the co-op was dissolved in 1905, it reopened as a residential hotel and has since become famous as the home---permanent or temporary---of people from all the creative fields, including musicians, writers, painters and actors.

The most prominent exterior feature of this Victorian-Gothic hotel is its delicate castiron balconies with their interlaced sunflower design stretching across the facade. The Chelsea was the first New York apartment building to reach 12 stories and the first to feature a penthouse. It has 400 rooms with permanent residents occupying about one half of the space.

From the beginning of its life as a hotel, it attracted an artistic clientele drawn by the noise-resistant space in which to work and play (the walls are three feet thick in most rooms). Artists of every esthetic persuasion have passed through here, many covering the walls with samples of their work.

Its earliest residents and visitors included **Mark Twain, O. Henry, William Dean Howells**, and **Sarah Bernhardt**. Later came **Thomas Wolfe**, who occupied an eighth floor corner suite in 1937, and poet **Edgar Lee Masters** who was also living here in that time. Writers **Eugene O'Neill, James T. Farrell, Tennessee Williams, Mary McCarthy**, and **Nelson Algren** came in the following years.

In 1953, poet **Dylan Thomas**, resident of Room 205, left the hotel one night for a drink and returned after downing 18 straight whiskeys. He soon lapsed into a fatal coma. In the early 1960's, dramatist **Brendan Behan** wrote his last works here while usually in an alcoholic haze.

Arthur Miller lived at the Chelsea from 1962 until 1968, after his marriage to **Marilyn Monroe**, and wrote *After the Fall* here. Science fiction writer **Arthur C. Clarke** made this his home on and off for a number of years and wrote his novel, *2001: A Space Odyssey*, in a 10th floor apartment. **Bob Dylan** wrote his rock song *"Sad-Eyed Lady of the Lowlands"* while staying here, and it was here that **William Burroughs** wrote *Naked Lunch*.

By the late 60's, the Chelsea became a popular spot for rock bands (and their groupies) passing through New York, including **Jimi Hendrix, Janis Joplin**, and the **Grateful Dead**, the **Mamas and the Papas**, and **Jefferson Airplane**.

Actress **Jane Fonda**, and film directors **Milos Forman** and **Peter Brook** spent time here. **Andy Warhol** used the hotel for a scene in his movie, *Chelsea Girls*, here in 1966.

Jackson Pollock, Willem de Kooning, and **Larry Rivers** are only a few of the many painters who have lived at the Chelsea. Probably its most prominent musician was **Virgil Thomson** who lived here in a ninth floor apartment for more than 40 years.

9/ William Saroyan
221 W. 23rd St. between Seventh and Eighth Avenue.

In the summer of 1928, the **Pulitzer Prize**-winning playwright from San Francisco came to New York City. He was 20 years old and just becoming a writer. When his bus arrived at the depot, he discovered that his suitcase with most of his money was missing, and he was stranded in the middle of the night with less than $2 in his pocket. Wandering a couple of blocks downtown, he found himself in front of this old **YMCA** building, across from the **Chelsea Hotel**, and it was here that he moved in for a short stay. He soon bought a portable Corona typewriter for $60, started to write, and explored the city. In January of 1929, suffering from a bout of homesickness, he returned to San Francisco.

10/ Vincent "Mad Dog" Coll
314 W. 23rd St. between Eighth and Ninth Avenue.

Coll was a vicious young mobster and killer during the Prohibition era whose gang was engaged in a long-running war against **Dutch Schultz**, another powerful New York organized crime leader.

Coll was living in a rooming house a few blocks from here on February 8, 1932, when Schultz finally caught up with him. Coll went into a phone booth in a drugstore in this building. Schultz's killers waited until he close the door, then riddled him with submachine bullets. He died instantly.

The drugstore is gone; the building now houses an oriental restaurant.

11/ John O'Hara
470 W. 24th St. near Tenth Avenue.

In the fall of 1937, **O'Hara** lived in this gigantic apartment complex called **London Terrace**. It was here that he finished his novel, *Hope of Heaven*. He kept this apartment for some time afterwards and sublet it when he was out of New York.

These **London Terrace Apartments**, made up of 14 buildings and 1,670 apartments, take up the entire block between Ninth and Tenth Avenue and were built in 1930.

12/ Clement Clarke Moore
435 W. 23rd St. between Ninth and Tenth Avenue.

Moore, who grew up in a mansion just southwest of the corner of 23rd Street and Eighth Avenue in the late 18th century, is the man credited with beginning the development of **Chelsea** when he divided his estate into lots around the year 1830.

He is better known as the author of the Christmas poem *"A Visit from St. Nicholas."* The original stone of Moore's house is displayed here on the steps at 435 W. 23rd St., at the south side of the **London Terrace** apartments.

13/ Edwin Arlington Robinson
450 W. 23rd St. between Ninth and Tenth Avenue.

The Italianate rowhouses on this block are now nicely renovated but in 1901 when the poverty-stricken poet moved into a dingy cubicle here, they were crumbling brownstones. The owner of this house at 450 W. 23rd, in gratitude for a personal favor, told **Robinson** to take the room and pay the rent whenever he felt like it. He lived here until 1905, much of the time spent alone drinking and writing. During that period, he sold not a line of poetry. Visiting friends could see him from the street in his top floor window, sitting in the hall bedroom. A neighbor in the adjoining room could hear the creak of his rocker late in the night; what he was doing was composing on his little pad, pursuing his calling.

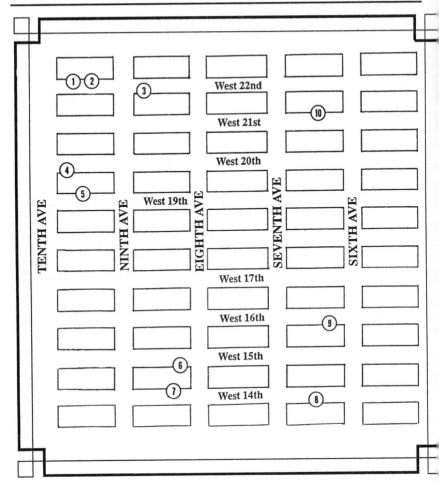

Tour 2

1/ Geraldine Page
2/ Sherwood Anderson
3/ Malcolm Cowley
4/ Jack Kerouac
5/ Edna St. Vincent Millay

6/ James Agee
7/ Orson Welles
8/ Woody Guthrie
9/ Edmund Wilson
10/ Jack Kerouac

Tour 2

1/ Geraldine Page
435 W. 22nd St. between Ninth and Tenth Avenue.

The stage and movie actress lived in an apartment in this building during the last years of her life. She died of a heart attack here in June 1987.

2/ Sherwood Anderson
427 W. 22nd St. between Ninth and Tenth Avenue.

The author of *Winesburg Ohio* lived in a cheap room in this rowhouse in 1918. A friend had obtained a job for him as a publicity man for a movie company at a salary of $75 a week but he spent most of his time here writing his novel, *Poor White*. "It was a good room," he wrote in his memoirs, recalling that he was at the back of the house, high enough up to look across many back yards and into other people's rooms. He wrote that after dark he could turn off his lights and sit by his window to observe people dining, quarreling, and making love. The result of his observations, he said, was that he saw a good deal of the inside of the lives of many people.

3/ Malcolm Cowley
360 W. 22nd St. at Ninth Avenue.

Cowley, one of America's best literary historians, critics and editors, lived in a top-floor, two-room studio apartment on this site from the early 1930's until November 1935. Cowley was then literary editor of *The New Republic* and during that time he married his second wife, **Muriel Mauer**. Their son was born in that period. They left to take a larger apartment in Greenwich Village. Their building has been replaced by the modern apartments you see.

Kerouac

4/ Jack Kerouac
454 W. 20th St. near Tenth Avenue.

Kerouac moved into an apartment in this red brick rowhouse with his second wife, **Joan Haverty**, in January 1951. Here he struggled to write the novel, *On the Road*. Stymied by his inability to sustain a free flow of words and distracted by the need to keep putting fresh pages in his typewriter, he got the idea, in early April, of taping together 20-foot strips of Japanese drawing paper to form a roll that could be fed continuously through his typewriter. For the next 20 days, he typed almost nonstop at his kitchen table, sleeping rarely, and had most of his book finished by April 25. Kerouac and Joan separated in June, and he moved away to a friend's apartment.

5/ Edna St. Vincent Millay
449 W. 19th St. between Ninth and Tenth Avenue.

In January of 1919, the poet, with her mother and two sisters, moved into a cheap tenement apartment on this site where a modern brick apartment building now stands. She was living here in this poor neighborhood when she first met **Edmund Wilson**, who later became her lover and biographer. Wilson later recalled that when he would go to get her at her apartment or take her home in a cab, the poor children playing in the street would run up and crowd around her. Sometimes she gave them pennies and sometimes taxi-rides, but it especially was the magnetism that we all felt, he wrote. **Millay** stayed here until September, 1920, when she moved to Greenwich Village.

6/ James Agee
322 W. 15th St. between Eighth and Ninth Avenue.

In late 1939, the writer moved into an apartment here with his second wife, **Alma**. It was a neighborhood surrounded by bars and factories and they lived above a bar where the jukebox played nothing but *"Roll Out the Barrel."* Badly needing money, **Agee** took a job as a book reviewer for *Time*

Magazine. His son, **Joel**, was born in 1940. With their marriage going badly, Alma took the child and moved out in 1941. Agee himself moved away soon after.

7/ Orson Welles
319 W. 14th St. between Eighth and Ninth Avenue.

The famed actor-director was only 20 when he moved into a small basement apartment here on the outskirts of Greenwich Village in 1935 with his first wife, **Virginia Nicolson**. The apartment was next to a Chinese laundry and a flophouse. He paid the $55 a month rent mainly by doing radio narration. It was during this period that he directed the famous all-black production of *Macbeth* for **Harlem's Negro Theater**. He then began to direct and perform in a series of successful productions for the **Federal Theater**. In 1937, **Welles** and his wife moved to a country home on the Hudson River outside New York City.

8/ Woody Guthrie
148 W. 14th St. between Sixth and Seventh Avenue.

The folksinger and songwriter lived in a room in this five-story building in 1942. He lived here with **Marjorie Mazia**, a dancer who later became his second wife.

It was here that **Guthrie** began to write his book, *Bound for Glory*, which was published in 1943.

9/ Edmund Wilson

114 W. 16th St. between Sixth and Seventh Avenue.

After his discharge from the army in August, 1919, the famous literary critic moved with friends into an apartment in this six-story white brick building. He lived here until 1921. During this period he became managing editor of the journal, *Vanity Fair*.

10/ Jack Kerouac

125 W. 21st St. between Sixth and Seventh Avenue.

In 1950, on the site of this parking lot stood a building where **Kerouac's** free-spirited friend, **Bill Cannastra**, lived. It was a loft located above a lampshade factory and the author of *On the Road* visited him here on and off during that year.

The apartment was the scene of many wild parties; one night, Cannastra ran naked around the block in the rain with **Kerouac** following in his shorts.

After Cannastra's premature death in a grisly subway accident, Kerouac moved into the loft with Cannastra's girlfriend, **Joan Haverty**, and married her soon afterward. By the end of the year they had left to live with Kerouac's mother.

Section Six:

Murray Hill and Surroundings

Pierpont Morgan Library

Site of the home of J. Pierpont Morgan

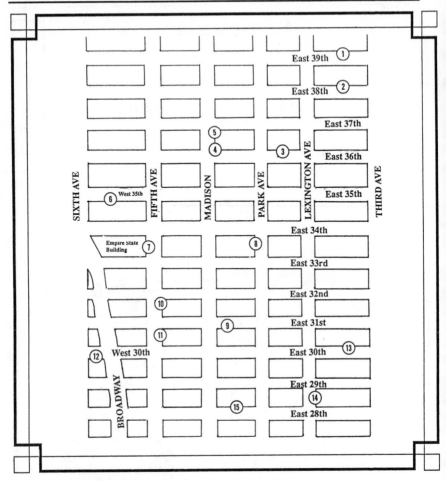

1/ F. Scott Fitzgerald
2/ Dashiell Hammett
3/ Franklin D. Roosevelt
4/ Pierpont Morgan
5/ J. P. Morgan, Jr.
6/ Eugene O'Neill
7/ Waldorf Astoria Hotel
8/ Enrico Caruso

9/ Henry Miller
10/ Sinclair Lewis
11/ Alfred Stieglitz
12/ Stephen Crane
13/ Dashiell Hammett
14/ William Randolph Hearst
15/ Mark Rothko

*Section Six covers the area which includes the **Murray Hill** neighborhood and the streets near it to the south and west. Its boundaries are **East 28th** to **East 42nd Street** and between **Third Avenue and Broadway**. Murray Hill itself (bounded roughly by **Madison** and **Third Avenues**, **34th** to **42nd Street**), although no longer the elegant place it was earlier in this century, is still a comfortable residential neighborhood. It became very fashionable in the mid-19th century as wealthy New Yorkers moved uptown, building brownstone mansions along Fifth, Madison, and Park Avenues. Murray Hill is named after **Robert Murray** who had a country estate here during the Revolutionary period. His house was at Park Avenue and 37th Street; it was here that Murray's wife is said to have served tea to **General Howe** and his staff while the Revolutionary troops escaped to the northwest. Although most of the great mansions are gone, a few outstanding brownstones and carriage houses remain to suggest this neighborhood's more elegant days--and to remind us that Murray Hill was the home of a number of famous New Yorkers.*

Tour 1

1/ F. Scott Fitzgerald
143 E. 39th St. between Lexington and Third Avenue.

On February 11, 1920, soon after he wrote *This Side of Paradise*, he moved into a room in this building, then called the **Allerton Hotel**. He had come to New York after spending a month in New Orleans working unsuccessfully on a novel. He and **Zelda Sayre** had just become engaged. Here at the Allerton, he began work on two of his best known short stories, *"The Jelly Bean"* and *"May Day."* Two months later he married Zelda in **St. Patrick's Cathedral**. This building is now numbered 145 and is the **Ten Eyck-Troughton Memorial Residence for Women.**

2/ Dashiell Hammett
133 E. 38th St. between Lexington and Third Avenue.

In the spring of 1931, the crime novelist moved to New York from California where he had been working as a screenwriter.

Broke, fed up with Hollywood, and drinking heavily, he took an apartment here in **Murray Hill** in this attractive building. He stayed until the end of 1931, working on a novel that would later become *The Thin Man.*

3/ Franklin D. and Eleanor Roosevelt
125 E. 36th St. between Park and Lexington Avenue.

The young couple moved into this beautiful five-story brownstone house in 1905 after their honeymoon in Europe.

Franklin spent his last two years at **Columbia Law School** during this time and started practicing law in 1907. While they lived here, their first two children, **Anna** and **James**, were born. They moved to the Upper East Side in the fall of 1908 (See Section Three, Tour 1, Number 7).

4/ Pierpont Morgan
219 Madison Ave. at 36th Street (north-east corner).

The Pierpont Morgan Library is probably Murray Hill's most notable landmark. On this site where the newer part of the library now stands, facing Madison Avenue, stood the home of the famous banking entrepreneur.

It was a large three-story brownstone mansion, and **Morgan** moved into it with his family in 1880. He lived here until his death in 1913 and built his library around the corner at 33 E. 36th St. in 1906.

Pierpont's son, **J.P. Morgan, Jr.**, had the mansion demolished in 1928 to make way for this new annex to the main library. This part of the library contains Morgan's entire private collection which was originally located on the first floor of the old mansion.

5/ J. P. Morgan, Jr.
231 Madison Ave. at 37th Street (southeast corner).

The banker son of **Pierpont Morgan** lived in this beautiful 45-room house from 1905 until his death in 1944. It is probably the last freestanding Italianate brownstone in Manhattan.

It was built in 1852 for the banker **Anson Phelps Stokes**. From 1944 to 1988 it was the headquarters of the **Lutheran Church in America**. Now owned by the **Morgan Library**, the house will be opened to the public after renovations are completed in 1991.

J. P. Morgan

6/ Eugene O'Neill
36 W. 35th St. between Broadway and Fifth Avenue.

O'Neill was a young and successful playwright when he took an apartment in this building in 1921 with his second wife, **Agnes Boulton**. Two of his most famous plays, *Anna Christie* and *The Hairy Ape* had their first productions while he was living here. The O'Neill's moved to Connecticut in the fall of 1922.

7/ Waldorf Astoria Hotel (original)
350 Fifth Ave. between 33rd and 34th Street.

Here, on the spot where the **Empire State Building** now stands, was the legendary **Waldorf Astoria Hotel**. It was built in 1893 as the result of a rivalry between two branches of the **Astor** family.

William Waldorf Astor, who owned a large home on the northwest corner of 33rd Street, was piqued at the prominent social position of his aunt, **Mrs. William Astor**, who lived next to him at the southwest corner of 34th Street. In order to arouse her wrath, he razed his home and built the large **Waldorf Hotel** on this site in 1893.

Mrs. Astor angrily moved uptown to East 65th Street. In 1897, after the two families had smoothed over their differences, the Astors built the **Astoria Hotel** and connected it with the Waldorf to create the **Waldorf Astoria**. This grandiose 17-story red brick and sandstone landmark soon became one of the world's greatest hotels. Its **Waldorf Bar** functioned as an exclusive men's club catering to the likes of **Morgan, Frick, Carnegie**, and **Guggenheim**. The Waldorf Astoria was demolished in 1929. The new Waldorf Astoria, at 50th and Park, opened in 1931 (See Section Two, Tour 4, Number 13).

8/ Enrico Caruso
4 Park Ave. at 34th Street.

This apartment building was erected in 1912 as the **Hotel Vanderbilt**. Caruso moved here in 1920 after living at the **Knickerbocker Hotel** for 12 years. The Vanderbilt was his last New York home. He went to Italy in 1921 and died soon afterwards.

9/ Henry Miller
28 E. 31st St. at Madison Avenue.

The author lived in an apartment here for a few months in early 1935. The building was known as the **Roger Williams Apartments**. **Miller** was in love with writer **Anais Nin** at the time and had traveled to New York from his home in France to visit her (see Section One, Tour 3, Number 9). He was staying here when he finished his novel, *Black Spring*. Miller returned to France in the summer of 1935.

10/ Sinclair Lewis
309 Fifth Ave. between 31st and 32nd Street.

In 1917, **Lewis**, as a young, struggling writer lived in a small apartment on this site with his first wife, **Grace**. Learning that she was pregnant, and in need of money, Lewis began to write short stories at a rapid rate. He published 44 in all during the next two years. *Main Street*, the novel that made him famous, appeared in 1920. The old apartment building here has been replaced by this modern building.

11/ Alfred Stieglitz
291 Fifth Ave. between 30th and 31st Street.

On this site where the huge **Textile Building** now stands, **Stieglitz** opened his famous **"291" Gallery** for the purpose of displaying the works of those photographers turned down by other New York galleries because their work stood above the commercial standards of the time.

The year was 1905 and the small gallery, formerly the studio of fellow photographer **Edward Steichen**, soon widened its scope to include the works of painters and sculptors. Masters of the new art movement in Europe-- **Cezanne, Picasso, Matisse, Rodin**-- had their first American representation at the 291 Gallery.

Stieglitz's gallery stayed open until 1917. The building was demolished in 1919 and this building replaced it in 1921.

12/ Stephen Crane
42 W. 30th St. between Broadway and Sixth Avenue.

Crane was a young journalist in 1893 when he met an artist named **Corwin Linson** who had a studio in this old four-story building.

Crane stayed with Linson off and on during that year and it was in Linson's studio that he worked on his novels *The Red Badge of Courage* and *Maggie: A Girl of the Streets.*

13/ Dashiell Hammett
155 E. 30th St. between Lexington and Third Avenue.

In the fall of 1929, the detective writer left San Francisco for good, coming to New York with woman friend, **Nell Martin.**

They lived together in an apartment on this site. **Hammett** and Martin separated after a few months but he stayed here, awaiting the publication of his new novel, *The Maltese Falcon*, and writing his next one, *The Glass Key*, which he finally finished in one continuous 30-hour writing session. Ham-

mett moved to Hollywood in 1930 to write for the movies.

Hearst

14/ William Randolph Hearst
123 Lexington Ave. near 28th Street.

In 1900, the millionaire publisher, as a young bachelor, moved into this four-story brownstone house. He filled it with all of the art objects he had collected from his many European trips.

This was the same house owned earlier by **President Chester Arthur**. He took the oath of office here after **James Garfield** was assassinated on September 20, 1881.

Marion Davies remembers being arrested at the age of 10 for throwing rotten fruit at **Hearst's** house on Halloween night. Years later, Davies became Hearst's mistress. By 1907, with a wife, two children, and a growing art collection, Hearst found that this house was too small for him, and he rented a huge apartment at the **Clarendon** on 137 Riverside Drive. (See Section Four, Tour 4, Number 8.)

15/ Mark Rothko
29 E. 28th St. between Madison and Park Avenue.

The abstract expressionist painter lived in this red brick apartment house with his first wife, **Edith Sachar**, from 1940 until 1943. He was just then becoming famous in the art world--his first one-man exhibition took place in 1944.

Section Seven:

Gramercy Park and Surroundings

34 Gramercy Park East

Home of James Cagney

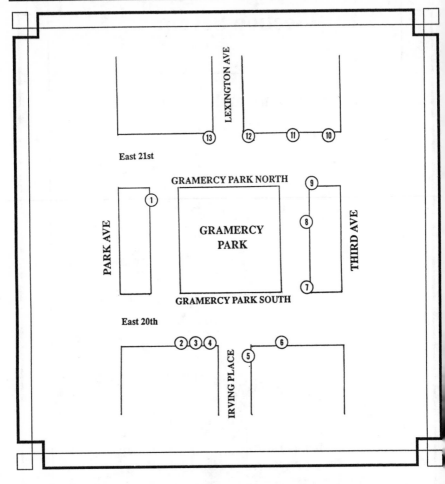

Tour 1

1/ John Garfield
2/ Samuel Tilden
3/ Edwin Booth
4/ Joseph Pulitzer
5/ Norman Thomas
6/ Thomas Edison
7/ James Cagney

8/ John Barrymore
9/ John Steinbeck
10/ Norman Thomas
11/ Hart Crane
12/ Cyrus Field
13/ Gramercy Park Hotel

Gramercy Park *and its surrounding neighborhood is one of New York's most charming sections and certainly one of the parts of the city which most recalls the past. This section covers an area from* **East 16th Street** *to* **East 27th Street** *and between* **Broadway** *and* **First Avenue**. *Change has come slowly here; many of the houses and apartment buildings date from the 19th century. Over the years it has been the home of countless prominent New Yorkers, many of them artists and writers.*

Gramercy Park *itself (Tour 1) is much like a London square. Laid out at the end of* **Lexington Avenue** *between* **20th** *and* **21st Streets** *in 1831 by a developer who sold off building lots around the park, it is the city's only private residential square. The park is still beautifully maintained by its owners, those who live in the buildings facing the square and who are the only ones with keys to its iron gates. Gramercy Park has retained its 19th century charm. Except for the construction done on the north side of the square in the 1920's, there have been relatively few alterations in this century*

Tour 1

1/ John Garfield
3 Gramercy Park West.

Built in 1846, this beautiful Greek Revival house with cast iron verandas, was the young actor's last home. He was living here with a friend, **Iris Whitney**, owner of the house, when he died in his sleep on May 19, 1952. He had been starring in the Broadway revival of *Golden Boy* at the time of his death. He was only 39 years old.

2/ Samuel Tilden
15 Gramercy Park South.

This brownstone, built in 1845 and remodelled in the Gothic Revival style in 1874, was the home of New York Governor **Samuel Tilden**. Tilden is best remembered as the presidential candidate in 1876 who won the popular vote by 250,000 but lost in the electoral college to Republican **Rutherford B.**

Hayes. This building became the **National Arts Club** in 1906. Among its many prominent members over the years have been **George Bellows, Alfred Stieglitz, Frederic Remington, Woodrow Wilson,** and **Theodore Roosevelt**.

3/ Edwin Booth
16 Gramercy Park South.

Booth, who was the greatest American actor of the 19th century and older brother of the man who assassinated **Abraham Lincoln**, purchased this house in 1888. He commissioned **Stanford White** to remodel it, and then turned it into the **Players Club**, which he presented to a group of New York actors as their permanent home. Booth died in his quarters here at the club on June 8, 1893. His statue stands across the street inside the park.

4/ Joseph Pulitzer
17 Gramercy Park South.

When the publisher moved from St. Louis to New York in 1883 to take over the ownership of the New York World, he leased this red brick house. He lived here with his wife, **Kate**, and their young family until 1885 when he moved uptown to Fifth Avenue. No. 17 Gramercy Park is now owned by the **Salvation Army**.

5/ Norman Thomas
20 Gramercy Park S. at Irving Place.

Thomas, the man who ran for president six times between 1928 and 1948 as the **Socialist Party** candidate, lived here with his wife between 1941 and 1945 after the last of their children had left the family house at 206 E. 18th St. (see this section, Tour 3, Number 8).

6/ Thomas Edison
24 Gramercy Park S.

The inventor was only 34 years old but already world famous and very wealthy when he rented an apartment on this site with his wife, **Mary**, and their young daughter, **Marion**, in the winter of 1881. Mary sent out cards inviting people to tea-and-champagne, though **Edison**, who detested such parties, never appeared at them. His laboratory was located in upper Manhattan. The Edisons used their house in Menlo Park as their summer home for the next two years, living here in Gramercy Park during the other months. The original house was demolished in 1908 and replaced by this modern building.

Booth

7/ James Cagney
34 Gramercy Park E.

Built in 1883, this red brick Victorian apartment house called the **Gramercy** is probably the city's first cooperative. **Cagney** was only one of the prominent actors to live here over the years. Actress **Margaret Hamilton** who played the wicked witch in the movie, *The Wizard of Oz*, made this her New York home. Others were **John Carradine**, and **Mildred Dunnock**. The building has the added distinction of having one of the city's few remaining cable-controlled bird cage elevators.

8/ John Barrymore
36 Gramercy Park E.

The actor lived in this building with his first wife, **Katherine Harris**. The apartment had a balcony overlooking the park. According to biographer, **Hollis Alpert**, the couple's loud and frequent quarrels caused neighboring tenants to write a joint letter of complaint to their landlord. As the tenants marched out of the building to mail the letter, they noticed the **Barrymores** walking arm-in-arm in Gramercy Park, cooing and chattering away like doves. They hadn't the heart to mail the letter. Barrymore and Harris were divorced in 1916.

9/ John Steinbeck
38 Gramercy Park N.

Steinbeck was a young writer just arrived from California in 1925 when he rented a small, dingy room in this building. It was up six flights of stairs and cost him $7 a week. He obtained a job as a cub reporter for the *New York World,* which supported him temporarily while he wrote short stories. After he was fired from the newspaper, he holed up in his room, writing day and night and living on little more than a few cans of sardines and a box of crackers. After his unsuccessful attempts to publish his stories, Steinbeck, dejected, returned to California in the summer of 1926.

10/ Norman Thomas
39-A Gramercy Park N.

Thomas lived alone in a small apartment on this site from 1949 until the early 1950's, after the death of his wife, **Violet.** He moved in soon after he ran for the presidency for the last time in 1948.

11/ Hart Crane
44 Gramercy Park N.

The young poet rented two rooms in an apartment on this site with his mother and grandmother in the summer of 1917. **Crane** was just getting his first poems published in magazines at this time.

12/ Cyrus Field
50 Gramercy Park N. at Lexington Ave.

Field, the man responsible for the laying of the first transatlantic telegraph cable in 1858, lived in a large house on this site for many years. The house was built in 1852 and demolished for the present building in 1909.

13/ Gramercy Park Hotel
2 Lexington Ave. at Gramercy Park North.

The **Gramercy Park Hotel** stands today on this corner where architect **Stanford White's** famous and beautiful house once stood (at 121 E. 21st St.). White's house was demolished in 1923 and a residential hotel, **Fifty-two Gramercy Park North** (now the **Gramercy Park Hotel**), was built and opened on the site in 1925.

Humphrey Bogart was a young actor when he married his first wife, **Helen Mencken**, at the hotel in 1926. She had an apartment here and the couple lived in it for a short period after the wedding. They were divorced in 1927.

Joseph P. Kennedy and his family rented the second floor of the hotel for a few months in the 1920's. **John F. Kennedy** was a young boy at the time and often played in Gramercy Park.

Critic **Edmund Wilson** and his wife, novelist **Mary McCarthy**, lived here in the early 1940's. In October 1979, humorist **S. J. Pereman** died in his apartment (Room 1621) here at the age of 75. Actress **Siobhan McKenna** made this hotel her New York home until her death in 1986.

Tour 2

1/ Theodore Roosevelt
28 E. 20th St. between Broadway and Park Ave.

T he 26th President of the United States was born here in 1858 on the site where this Greek Revival house (a replica of the original) now stands. He lived here until 1872 when his family took him to Europe to live. The original house was demolished in 1916 and then rebuilt to its original specifications in 1923. Now a public museum, it is full of period furniture and **Roosevelt** memorabilia.

2/ Gilbert and Sullivan
45 E. 20th St. between Broadway and Park Avenue

T hey visited New York in 1879 to conduct a performance of their operetta, *H.M.S. Pinafore.* During that time, **Sullivan** lived in a room in this building and on December 31, 1879, he finished writing the music for *The Pirates of Penzance.* Later that night he conducted its first performance to great acclaim.

Roosevelt

3/ David O. Selznick
270 Park Ave. S. at East 21st Street (northwest corner).

F rom 1916 until the early 1920's, the famous motion picture producer, best known for his production of *Gone With The Wind,* lived in this large build-

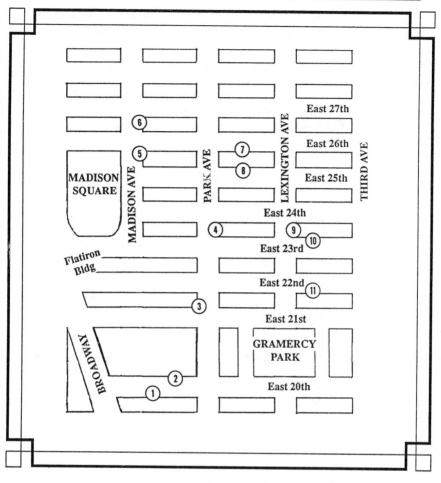

Tour 2

1/ Theodore Roosevelt

2/ Gilbert and Sullivan

3/ David Selznick

4/ Isadora Duncan

5/ Stewart and Fonda

6/ Madison Square Garden

7/ Herman Melville

8/ Henry James

9/ W.H. Auden

10/ Nathaniel West

11/ Cole Porter

ing as a teenager with his family. **Selznick's** father, **Lewis**, was a successful movie company owner and they rented a lavish, 22-room apartment complete with servants and chauffeured Rolls Royce. By 1926, the elder Selznick had lost most of his fortune and **David**, without money, moved to California to begin his own career in the movies. After a few years, he organized his own studio.

4/ Isadora Duncan

303 Fourth Ave. (Park Avenue) at 23rd Street (northeast corner).

T he free-spirited dancer lived and operated a studio here at this corner building from November 1914 until May 1915. She furnished it with blue curtains and low divans. She christened the place *"The Dionysian"* and brought in a small group of students to learn modern dance.

5/ James Stewart and Henry Fonda

37 Madison Ave. at 26th Street (southeast corner).

T he old **Madison Square Hotel** was located on the site where this government building stands. From 1933 to 1935, **Stewart** and **Fonda**, then young and struggling actors, rented a pair of rooms together here. They spent their spare time assembling model airplanes. In December of 1933, they both landed roles in the Broadway play, *All Good Americans.* In the following year, Fonda got his first real notice in the hit play, *New Faces,* and he went on to star in *The Farmer Takes a Wife* in 1935.

He then went to Hollywood to play the same role in the movie and Stewart, who also received movie offers, joined him there in the same year.

6/ Madison Square Garden (original)

55 Madison Ave. between 26th and 27th Street.

O n this site where the **New York Life Insurance Company** building stands, was the original **Madison Square Garden**, designed by architect **Stanford White**.

It opened in 1890 and White had a private apartment in its towers. It was here on June 25, 1906, that he was shot to death in the roof garden restaurant by Pittsburgh millionaire, **Harry Thaw**, whose wife, **Evelyn Nesbit**, had carried on a well-publicized affair with White. The old Madison Square Garden was demolished in 1925.

7/ Herman Melville

104 E. 26th St. between Park and Lexington Avenue.

T he author of *Moby Dick* lived in a small house on this site with his wife and four children from 1863 until his death in 1891. From 1866 to 1885 he worked for the **New York Custom House**. It was here that he wrote the novelette, *Billy Budd*, completing it in 1891, just five months before his death. The office building on the site of the **Melville** home is next to the huge **Regiment Armory Building**, site of the famous "Armory Show" of 1913, where Americans saw post-Impressionist paintings from Europe for the first time.

8/ Henry James
111 E. 25th St. between Park and Lexington Avenue.

In a house on this site, directly behind Melville's, **James** rented two rooms in January, 1875, and settled down to work on his first novel, *Roderick Hudson*. He was 31 years old. James lived here until July of that same year when he left New York for Europe where he lived for the rest of his life. The house was demolished in 1905 to make way for the Regiment Armory Building.

9/ W. H. Auden and Christopher Isherwood
23 Lexington Ave. between 23rd and 24th Street.

The two British writers moved from England to the U.S. in January, 1939, and found a temporary first home here at the 15-story **George Washngton Hotel**, which offered cheap rooms to long-staying guests.

10/ Nathaniel West
145 E. 23rd St. near Lexington Avenue.

In 1927 and 1928, the author of *Day of the Locust* was the assistant manager here at what is now called the **Hotel Kenmore**. It was then the Kenmore Hall Hotel. He was 24 years old and obtained the job through family connections. He spent his working nights here reading. Soon he began giving rooms to needy friends, some of them writers --a practice he continued when he worked at the **Hotel Sutton** later in 1928. (See Section Two, Tour 2, Number 14.)

Before the Kenmore was built, this was the site of a building where **Stephen Crane** lived as a young, struggling author.

He shared a small studio here in 1893 with three friends. They were so poor that they only had clothes enough for one of them at a time to go out looking for work. Crane worked on his novel, *The Red Badge of Courage*, while he lived here.

11/ Cole Porter
134 E. 22nd St. between Lexington and Third Avenue.

The famous song writer was 23 and a recent Yale graduate in 1916 when he rented an apartment on this site.

During the period he attempted to study serious musical composition with the distinguished teacher, **Pietro Yon**. Not taking his studies very seriously, **Porter** spent most of his time here as a host of numerous parties. When war was declared in 1917, Porter went to France to do volunteer relief work.

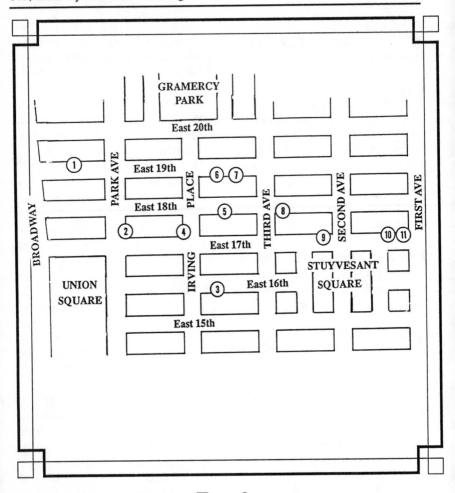

Tour 3

1/ Horace Greeley
2/ Theodore Dreiser
3/ Winslow Homer
4/ O. Henry
5/ Elinor Wylie
6/ Theda Bara

7/ George Bellows
8/ Norman Thomas
9/ William Dean Howells
10/ Charles Murphy
11/ Antonin Dvorak

Tour 3

1/ Horace Greeley
35 E. 19th St. between Broadway and Park Avenue.

This three-story building, dating from the 1850's, was an early home of the famous journalist and presidential candidate. Perhaps to preserve a little of the rural atmosphere he was used to, **Greeley** kept a goat in the back yard.

2/ Theodore Dreiser
201 Park Ave. S. at 17th Street (northeast corner).

Here, in the **Guardian Life Insurance Building** (across the street from **Union Square**), **Dreiser** rented a small office in January, 1925, and finished writing his novel, *An American Tragedy.* He was living then in Brooklyn with his companion, **Helen Richardson**. When Dreiser's novel was published at the end of 1925, it became a great popular success and, after years of financial struggle, he became rich.

3/ Winslow Homer
128 E. 16th St. between Irving Place and Third Avenue.

In 1859, the painter was 23 years old when he moved from Boston to New York and lived in a room in this five-story brick house. **Homer** remained here for two years and sold a few drawings to Harper's Weekly. In 1861, when the Civil War began, he became that magazine's military artist, traveling with the Union armies and sketching scenes from the camps and the battlefields.

4/ O. Henry
55 Irving Place near 17th Street.

The short-story writer rented the huge parlor and the alcove above it in this narrow four-story brownstone, from 1903 until 1907 (the plaque in front incorrectly claims he lived here from 1902-1910.) The main room was on the first floor, just to the left of the front entrance. He wrote many of his most famous stories while he lived alone here, including *"The Gift of the Magi."* The building now houses a restaurant. **O. Henry** often wrote and drank at **Healy's Cafe**, now **Pete's Tavern**, which still stands at the corner of Irving Place and 18th Street.

O. Henry

5/ Elinor Wylie and William Rose Benet

142 E. 18th St. between Irving Place and Third Avenue.

The two poets moved to an apartment on this site (where a modern apartment building now stands) soon after their marriage in 1923. **Wylie** was 38; it was her third marriage. They lived on this block for one year. Their apartment building was similar to the one still standing across the street at 143 E. 18th St.

6/ Theda Bara

132 E. 19th St. between Irving Place and Third Avenue.

The famous silent screen actress lived in this seven-story studio building. It was constructed without kitchens because most of the people there were never expected to eat in. **Ethel Barrymore, Helen Hayes**, and **Lillian** and **Dorothy Gish** also lived on this block at one time.

7/ George Bellows

146 E. 19th St. between Irving Place and Third Avenue.

The painter purchased this red brick house in 1910. He moved in with his new wife, **Emma**, and used the third floor as his studio. Later he would take his two young daughters to Gramercy Park, just around the corner, to skip rope and play with the neighborhood children.

Bellows was only 42 when he died of a ruptured appendix, while living at this house, in 1925.

8/ Norman Thomas

206 E. 18th St. at Third Avenue.

Thomas, who ran for president six times as the **Socialist Party** candidate, purchased this four-story house in 1923 and lived here with his wife and five children. It was their home until 1939.

9/ William Dean Howells

241 E. 17th St. between Second and Third Avenue.

The novelist who wrote *The Rise of Silas Lapham* lived with his wife and daughter in this well-preserved brownstone in the early 1890's. The house is directly opposite **Stuyvesant Square.**

Howells took daily walks in the Gramercy neighborhood and it was from his observations of people in all walks of life that he was able to write *A Hazard of New Fortunes* in 1890-- probably the first novel to offer a realistic view of New York.

10/ Charles Murphy

305 E. 17th St. between First and Second Avenue.

"Boss" Charles Murphy was New York City's most powerful political figure in the early years of this century as the leader of the Democratic Party's **Tammany Hall.** For many years he lived in a house on this site where a part of the **Beth Israel Medical Center** now stands. Murphy died in the house in 1924.

11/ Antonin Dvorak

327 E. 17th St. between First and Second Avenue.

The great Czech composer lived with his family in this old house while he was in New York City from 1892 until 1895.

He was appointed the head of the city's **National Conservatory of Music** in 1892. **Dvorak** wrote the symphony *"From the New World"* in 1893 while he was here.

Overcome by homesickness, he returned to Bohemia in 1895.

Section Eight:

Greenwich Village

Patchin Place

Home of e.e. cummings

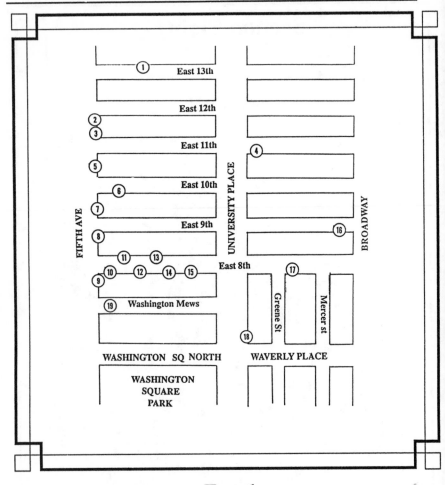

East 13th

East 12th

East 11th

East 10th

East 9th

East 8th

FIFTH AVE

UNIVERSITY PLACE

BROADWAY

Washington Mews

Greene St

Mercer st

WASHINGTON SQ NORTH

WAVERLY PLACE

WASHINGTON
SQUARE
PARK

Tour 1

1/ Anais Nin
2/ Al Smith
3/ Marlon Brando
4/ Thomas Wolfe
5/ Walter Lippmann
6/ John Garfield
7/ Mabel Dodge
8/ Mark Twain
9/ Sara Teasdale
10/ Barbara Hutton

11/ Thomas Wolfe
12/ Max Eastman
13/ John Cheever
14/ E.B. White
15/ Alger Hiss
16/ Lillian Russell
17/ Jackson Pollock
18/ Clifford Odets
19/ Washington Mews

Greenwich Village's borders run from West Houston Street to 13th Street and from Broadway to West Street. In the minds of most people, the Village stands for the unconventional. The impression starts with its physical environment---the buildings are lower than in the rest of Manhattan and the streets are narrow, crooked, and often intertwined. It has always been a place of refuge---a unique quarter unlike its surroundings, where others came to escape or to find something different. In its earliest days it was a favorite summer vacation spot for the wealthy. In the first decades of the 19th century it became a haven for people fleeing the yellow fever epidemic which swept through Lower Manhattan. Later its tenements and brownstones housed the great waves of European immigrants, especially the Irish and the Italians. By the turn of this century, the Village finally acquired its strongest present-day image when it became the home of New York's avant garde---artists, writers, musicians, theater people, and political and social radicals. Although times have obviously changed, many of its old and famous buildings still stand. They housed some of New York's most memorable people.

Tour 1

1/ Anais Nin
17 E. 13th St. between Fifth Avenue and University Place.

This small, two-story house was one of the two places where **Nin** published her own books. In 1942, frustrated by the indifference of commercial publishers to her work, she borrowed $175 from her friends, bought an old printing press, and rented a loft with her friend, **Gonzalo More**, at 144 MacDougal St., across from the Provincetown Playhouse. There they cut paper, set type, and proceeded to print three of Nin's books. Then, in April 1944, desiring a more businesslike atmosphere, they moved with the printing press into this building which now houses the **Erskine Press**. The loft on MacDougal Street has been demolished and replaced by a **New York University** building.

2/ Al Smith
51 Fifth Ave. at East 12th Street (southeast corner).

New York's famous Democratic governor moved to a penthouse apartment here in 1928 after he lost the presidential election to **Herbert Hoover**. The building is directly across the street from the **First Presbyterian Church**. **Smith** became the president of the newly built **Empire State Building** while he lived here and held the position for a number of years. He moved out of Greenwich Village in the early 1940's.

3/ Marlon Brando
43 Fifth Ave. at East 11th Street (northeast corner).

Brando, as a young actor, lived in a tiny apartment in this 11-story building in 1946. He shared it with an eccentric Russian violinist named **Igor**.

According to biographer **Charles Higham**, Brando enjoyed the Slav's company at first, but when he grew tired of him and wanted him to leave, he cut open the Russian's violin and filled it with horse manure. Igor departed.

4/ Thomas Wolfe
42 E. 11th St. at University Place (southeast corner).

This building was the **Hotel Albert** in the 1920's and it was the first New York residence of the novelist. He moved into Room 2220 in February, 1923, after he accepted a position as English instructor at nearby **New York University**. **Wolfe** lived here until the end of 1926.

5/ Walter Lippmann
39 Fifth Ave. between East 10th and 11th Street.

The journalist and political philosopher lived in an apartment here with his first wife, **Fay**, from 1926 until 1929. He was an editor for the *New York World* in that period.

6/ John Garfield
8 E. 10th St. near Fifth Avenue.

The young actor subleased a triplex apartment from his screenwriter friend, **Donald Ogden Stewart**, in this charming five-story house in 1947. It was the year he starred in his most famous film, *Body and Soul*.

7/ Mabel Dodge
23 Fifth Ave. between East 9th and 10th Street

The wealthy **Mrs. Dodge** rented a spacious apartment on the second floor of a four-story brownstone on this site in the years just before the First World War.

Here she received her radical and bohemian New York friends for Wednesday night gatherings that made her place the center of Village intellectual life and sexual intrigue.

Among the many famous who attended were **John Reed, Emma Goldman, Big Bill Haywood, Lincoln Steffens, Theodore Dreiser**, and **Max Eastman**. Dodge was John Reed's lover before he met **Louise Bryant**.

8/ Mark Twain
21 Fifth Ave. at East 9th Street (southeast corner).

He lived in a house on this site, now occupied by this large apartment complex, for four and one-half years between 1904 and 1908. **Twain** was 65 years old when he moved here.

He left New York for good in 1908 after the death of his daughter, **Jean**..

The house was demolished in 1954 along with the famous **Brevoort Hotel** which stood on this same block (at 11 Fifth Ave. and East 8th Street).

The Brevoort was a Greenwich Village landmark for a hundred years. Its basement cafe was a favorite attraction for the Village bohemian population.

Twain

9/ Sara Teasdale
1 Fifth Ave. at East 8th Street.

The poet moved into this apartment building in 1932. She was in poor health at the time, and it was here on January 30, 1933, that she committed suicide with an overdose of sleeping pills. She was 48 years old.

10/ Barbara Hutton
2 E. 8th St. at Fifth Avenue (southeast corner).

The socialite granddaughter of the founder of the **Woolworth** department stores lived in a mansion on this site as a child. She was only five when she moved away from here to live with her grandfather after her mother committed suicide in 1917. (See Section Three, Tour 6, Number 11.)

11/ Thomas Wolfe
13 E. 8th St. near Fifth Avenue.

The novelist shared a loft in an old building on this site with his lover, **Mrs. Aline Bernstein**, from 1926 until 1928. She split her time between **Wolfe** and her husband who lived on the Upper West Side. Wolfe's loft was a fourth floor room with a low, sloping ceiling and a skylight. It was here that he began the novel that made him famous, *Look Homeward, Angel*. The building was later demolished and replaced by these modern apartments.

12/ Max Eastman
12 E. 8th St. between University Place and Fifth Avenue.

Eastman, editor of the famous literary and political journal, *The Masses*, from 1912 until it was suppressed by the U.S. government in 1917, moved into a room on the second floor of these Tudor-style artists' quarters in 1917. It was the apartment of his friend, **Eugen Boissevain**, who later married **Edna St. Vincent Millay**. Eastman had just separated from his wife, **Ida Rauh**.

13/ John Cheever
19 E. 8th St. between University Place and Fifth Avenue.

The writer lived in a two-room apartment on this site just after his marriage to **Mary Winternitz** in 1941. He was 26 years old and by then regularly selling stories to the *New Yorker*. He joined the Armed Services soon after he moved here.

14/ E.B. White
16 E. 8th St. between University Place and Fifth Avenue.

The New Yorker essayist and his wife, editor **Katharine Angell White**, moved into an apartment in this house just after their marriage in 1930. It was a third-floor, three-room apartment. The Whites soon increased their living space by renting the apartment directly above them and connecting the two places by an interior stairway. It was their home until 1935.

15/ Alger Hiss
22 E. 8th St. between University Place and Fifth Avenue.

He was employed by the U.S. State Department when he moved into an apartment in this Tudor-style rowhouse with his wife, **Priscilla**, in 1947. He lived here until he was accused of being a Communist spy by **Whittaker Chambers** and convicted of perjury in the famous 1950 trial.

16/ Lillian Russell
58 E. 9th St. at Broadway.

The famous *"golden girl"* of the Gay Nineties and probably the country's most famous beauty at that time lived in a cozy and luxurious apartment on this site at the turn of the century. Here she was often picked up by the flamboyant playboy **Diamond Jim Brady** in a Hansom cab for a jaunt uptown to one of the popular night spots of that era. **Russell's** apartment building was replaced by this modern apartment building called the **Hamilton** (renumbered 60 East 9th Street).

17/ Jackson Pollock
46 E. 8th St. at Greene Street (southeast corner).

The abstract expressionist painter moved into a fifth-floor apartment and studio on this site in 1935. At that same time, he began to work for the **WPA Federal Art Project**, an organization set up by the **Roosevelt** administration during the Depression to help artists. His teacher and mentor, artist **Thomas Hart Benton** lived just down the street at 10 E. 8th.

Pollock was living here in 1941 when he met his lifelong companion, painter **Lee Krasner**; they were married in 1945. In that year, they moved from here to a house on Long Island where they lived until Pollock's death in 1956. Pollock's apartment on this site was torn down in 1952 to make way for this modern building.

18/ Clifford Odets
1 University Place at Waverly Place.

Just before the opening of his first play, *Awake and Sing!*, **Odets** and his colleague from the Group Theater, **Harold Clurman**, left their small place on Horatio Street to live here, in a large modern apartment on the 19th floor of this building. They were both still short of money and the place was sparsely furnished.

Odets said "all I wanted was two clean rooms to live in, a phonograph, some records, and to buy things for a girl. Nothing more I wanted." Odets continued to make this place his New York residence throughout the 1930's, even after he became very successful, moved temporarily to Hollywood and married his first wife, actress **Louise Rainer**.

19/ Washington Mews
(From Fifth Avenue to University Place between East 8th Street and Washington Square North).

This charming cobbled alley is a well-known Village landmark.

On its north side are buildings which were converted from stables into residences. The houses on the south, built in the 1930's, are on the land that was part of the rear gardens of the mansions on **Washington Square North**.

Political journalist **Walter Lippmann** lived at 50 Washington Mews from 1923 until 1926.

Novelist **Sherwood Anderson** often stayed with his friend, **Mary Emmett**, who lived at 54 Washington Mews.

Tour 2

1/ Numbers One and Three
Washington Square North.

Numbers **One** and **Three** are part of the beautiful row of Greek Revival townhouses built in the early 1830's on the east side of **Washington Square North**. They have been the home of many artists and writers over the years.

Edith Wharton, William Dean Howells, and **Henry James** all lived and worked at **Number One**, at one time or another.

Number Three, called the *"Studio Building"* was the home of painter **Edward Hopper** from 1913 until his death in 1967. Literary critic **Edmund Wilson** lived here from 1921 until 1925 when he separated from his first wife, **Mary Blair**.

Novelist **John Dos Passos** rented the rear apartment on the first floor behind Number Three in 1922, where he wrote, painted pictures, and began plans for his novel, *Manhattan Transfer.*

2/ Edith Wharton
7 Washington Square North.

The novelist lived here in 1882 after she had returned from Europe with her mother. She was 20 years old. **Numbers 7-13** of this row have retained their original appearance but are one facade with the doors rarely used today. Alterations of the building have converted these once-separate houses into one private apartment house with an entrance on Fifth Avenue.

3/ Henry James, Cornelius Vanderbilt
21 Washington Place and 10 Washington Place near Greene Street.

Near this corner (where buildings of **New York University** now stand) lived perhaps America's greatest novelist and its most notorious businessman of the 19th century.

Henry James was born in 1843 in a house at 21 Washington Place. At 10

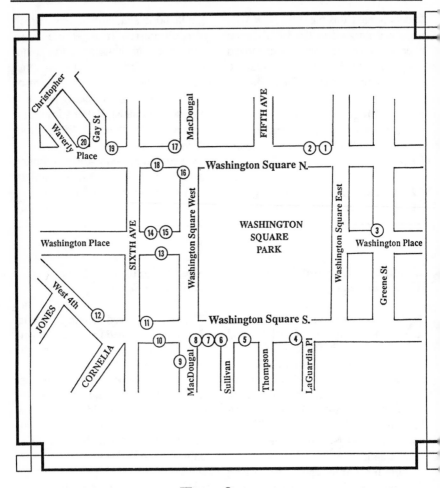

Tour 2

1/ Washington Square North
2/ Edith Wharton
3/ Henry James
4/ "House of Genius"
5/ Edwin Arlington Robinson
6/ Reed and Bryant
7/ John Reed
8/ Eugene O'Neill
9/ Provincetown Playhouse
10/ John Barrymore

11/ John Reed
12/ Bob Dylan
13/ Richard Wright
14/ Delmore Schwartz
15/ Diane Arbus
16/ Eleanor Roosevelt
17/ Bob Dylan
18/ Max Eastman
19/ Edna St. Vincent Millay
20/ Judy Holliday

Washington Place, railroad tycoon and robber baron **Cornelius Vanderbilt** resided in a four-story brick mansion from 1846 until his death in 1877.

Also at this site (as the plaque on the **NYU Brown Building** notes) on March 25, 1911, 146 people, most of them women, died in a fire at the **Triangle Shirtwaste Company,** in a building believed to be completely fireproof. This tragic event focused public attention on the dangerous conditions of the sweatshop and led to its ultimate reform.

4/ Number 61
Washington Square S. at LaGuardia Place.

One of **Greenwich Village's** most famous landmarks once stood on this corner. It was a roominghouse which residents referred to as the *"House of Genius."*

Here, at one time or another, lived a whole array of important American writers, including **Willa Cather, Stephen Crane, John Dos Passos, Theodore Dreiser, Frank Norris, O. Henry,** and **Eugene O'Neill**.

The old building was torn down in the late 1950's. The **Loeb Studio Center** of **New York University** stands here today.

5/ Edwin Arlington Robinson
55 Washington Square S. between Thompson and Sullivan Street.

The **Pulitzer Prize**-winning poet rented a room with a single window facing the rear, in the tower of this Jud-son Memorial Church in 1906. He was working at the U.S. Custom House on Wall Street---a job obtained for him by President Theodore Roosevelt.

6/ John Reed and Louise Bryant
43 Washington Square S. between Sullivan and MacDougal Street.

The young revolutionary journalist met **Louise Bryant** while on a speaking tour in Portland, Oregon in the winter of 1915. They swiftly became lovers and Bryant left her husband to come with **Reed** to New York. They moved into Reed's apartment on this site in January, 1916.

Reed was heavily involved in antiwar activity at that time. They were married in the fall of 1916. In August 1917, they left for Russia together to witness the Revolution.

7/ John Reed
42 Washington Square S. between Sullivan and MacDougal Street.

In the summer of 1911, **Reed** moved into a shabby apartment on the third floor of an old building on this site with three friends from Harvard. He was 23. It was his first residence in Greenwich Village.

Soon his friend and mentor, muckraking journalist **Lincoln Steffens**, recently widowed, moved into the apartment directly below Reed's.

By 1913, Reed had moved into **Mabel Dodge's** apartment at 23 Fifth Ave.

8/ Eugene O'Neill
*38 Washington Square S. near Mac-
Dougal Street.*

In the fall of 1916, the young playwright, just returned from Provincetown, Massachusetts, where his first play, *Bound East for Cardiff,* had been produced at the **Wharf Theater**, took a room in a building on this site. It was only a few doors away from **John Reed** and **Louise Bryant's** apartment. He was living here when he had a brief affair with Bryant, while Reed was in the hospital recovering from surgery.

9/ Provincetown Playhouse
133 MacDougal St. near Washington Square South.

In the fall of 1918, the **Provincetown Players** moved their famous theater into this remodeled four-story pre-Victorian building which had previously been, in turn, a storehouse, a stable, and a bottling works.

The Players had started as a summer theater on Cape Cod and became officially organized in New York City in 1916. Their first location before coming here was up the street at 139 MacDougal.

The Playhouse was a landmark in American theatrical history; it was not organized for monetary profit. Its primary object was to encourage the writing of plays of real artistic, literary and dramatic---as opposed to commercial---merit. **Eugene O'Neill** was its most famous member. His first play, *Bound East for Cardiff,* was performed by the Players in 1916.

Barrymore

10/ John Barrymore
132 W. 4th St. between MacDougal Street and Sixth Avenue.

Barrymore moved to the top floor of this old four-story house across from the **Washington Square United Methodist Church** in October, 1917, turning the attic into a bachelor retreat that he called the *"Alchemist's Corner."*

He decorated the walls with gold paper and proceeded to landscape the roof, bringing in tons of soil and planting large cedar trees. After the actor had moved out, a rain storm caused the roof to buckle and much of the heavy topsoil leaked into the rooms below.

11/ John Reed
147 W. 4th St. near Sixth Avenue.

In the fall of 1918, **Reed** took an attic room in this Italianate building (now housing the **Ristorante Volare**) to write his account of the Russian Revolution. Here, according to his friend **Max Eastman**, he worked 16 and 18 hours a day, red-eyed and unshaven, to finish *Ten Days That Shook the World.*

12/ Bob Dylan
161 W. 4th St. between Cornelia Street and Jones Street.

Dylan moved into a two-room apartment in this building in 1962. His place was on the rear first floor, over **Bruno's** spaghetti parlor and rented for about $60 a month.

In those days, he performed regularly at the legendary **Gerde's Folk City** on 11 W. 4th St. which was known as New York's center of folk music.

13/ Richard Wright, Willa Cather
82 Washington Place between Sixth Avenue and Washington Square West.

The black novelist moved into a four-room apartment on the third floor of this building with his wife, **Ellen**, and his daughter, **Julia**, in November, 1945, soon after his novel, *Black Boy,* was published. They stayed until 1947 when they purchased a house at 13 Charles St., a few blocks away.

Willa Cather, after being appointed managing editor of *McClure's Magazine* in 1908, moved into an apartment here with her long-time companion, **Edith Lewis**. They stayed until 1913. Cather wrote *Alexander's Bridge* during her stay here.

14/ Delmore Schwartz
73 Washington Place between Sixth Avenue and Washington Square West.

The poet was 24 years old when he moved into an attic loft in this building in 1937. The room could be reached only by climbing a ladder. **Schwartz** lived here until his first marriage in June, 1938, producing some of his best work during his stay.

15. Diane Arbus
71 Washington Place between Sixth Avenue and Washington Square West.

Arbus, with her husband, **Allen**, opened a new photography studio on the parlor floor of this (then) reconverted townhouse in 1958. They lived in the same building.

But their marriage was failing by then and Arbus moved out in the summer of 1959, taking her two daughters with her, to a nearby house at 121 1/2 Charles St. (See this section, Tour 5, Number 11).

16/ Eleanor Roosevelt
29 Washington Square West at Waverly Place (corner).

The former **First Lady** moved into this building in 1945, soon after the death of **Franklin**. She lived here until 1948 when she moved uptown.

17/ Bob Dylan
103 Waverly Place at MacDougal Street.

In 1961, **Dylan**, then only 20 and just arrived from Minneapolis, moved into this small hotel called the **Hotel Earle** (it's now the **Washington Square Hotel**). He began performing at various small bars and coffee houses in this neighborhood. He never stayed in one place very long. Before the end of the year, he moved to another place on Waverly, then to a tiny apartment on 161 W. Fourth St. near Sixth Avenue. (See Number 12 above.)

18/ Max Eastman
118 Waverly Place between Sixth Avenue and MacDougal Street.

Eastman, author and editor of the radical journal, *The Masses,* was a 26-year-old student at **Columbia University** when he moved into an apartment here in 1909. His sister, **Crystal Eastman**, writer, feminist, and social activist, lived with him. He stayed until 1911. Eastman became editor of *The Masses* in 1912 (see this section, Tour 3, Number 16). He moved back here to the same apartment in 1916 with his first wife, **Ida Rauh**.

19/ Edna St. Vincent Millay
139 Waverly Place between Gay Street and Sixth Avenue.

This was the first of four Greenwich Village residences of the famous poet. She was 25 when she moved into an "icy one and a half rooms" in this white brick building in 1917. Her sister, **Norma**, lived here with her. **Millay** was then acting and writing for the **Provincetown Players**. Their tiny apartment was just a few doors from where **Poe** wrote his poem *"Ligeia."*

20/ Judy Holliday
158 Waverly Place between Gay Street and Christopher Street.

In 1948, after her marriage to **David Oppenheim**, the actress moved into a large seven-room apartment on the top floor of this old red brick building. She was then appearing on Broadway in the role that made her a star, as **Billie Dawn** in *Born Yesterday.*

Their rooms here were furnished mainly with cast-off items---she was a great devotee of junk and furniture from second-hand stores. They lived here until the birth of their son in 1952 when they moved uptown to the **Dakota** on Central Park West.

Tour 3

1/ Jimi Hendrix
55 W. 8th St. near Sixth Avenue.

The rock guitarist made this turn-of-the-century apartment building one of his homes during the late 1960's. He redesigned and converted the rooms into his **Electric Lady Studio** where he recorded some of his records.

55 W. 8th St.
Home of Jimi Hendrix

2/ Jackson Pollock
9 MacDougal Alley near West 8th Street.

The painter, with his wife, **Lee,** stayed in the remodeled carriage house of a friend here in MacDougal Alley during the winters of 1949 and 1950. **Pollock,** famous by then, had come to New York for the exhibitions of his work at the **Parsons Gallery.** His

permanent home was in the town of Springs on Long Island.

3/ Edwin Arlington Robinson
28 W. 8th St. at MacDougal Street.

One morning in 1922, **Robinson** showed up here at the house of **James** and **Laura Fraser,** asking for temporary lodging. The three found living together so pleasant that he stayed here until 1927, living in a skylighted studio on the upper floor. The Frasers were both sculptors and understood the poet's need for privacy; Robinson felt completely at ease with them. They all moved together to 328 E. 42nd St. in 1927.

4/ Lenny Bruce
5 W. 8th St. between Fifth and Mac- Dougal Street.

The nightclub comedian lived in rooms on the second floor here at the **Marlton Hotel** in 1964 during his famous obscenity trial. **Bruce** was arrested in April of that year for giving an "obscene" performance at the **Cafe Au Go Go** in Greenwich Village.

He was found guilty in December after a long and highly publicized trial, and died less than two years later on August 3, 1966, in Hollywood. He was only 40 The poet **Delmore Schwartz** also lived here at the Marlton in 1956.

5/ James Thurber
8 Fifth Ave. at West 8th Street (southwest corner).

In 1935, soon after his divorce from his first wife, **Althea Adams, Thur-**

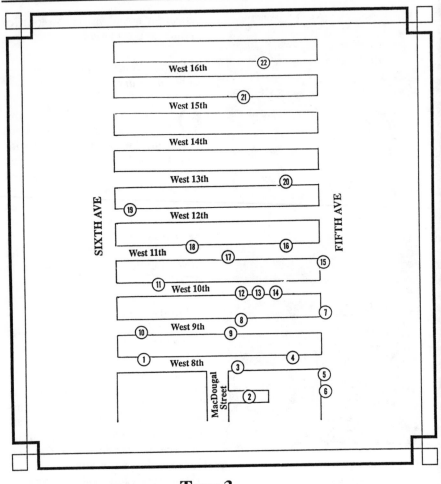

Tour 3

1/ Jimi Hendrix
2/ Jackson Pollock
3/ Edwin Arlington Robinson
4/ Lenny Bruce
5/ James Thurber
6/ Andre Kertesz
7/ Dashiell Hammett
8/ Marianne Moore
9/ Elinor Wylie
10/. S.J. Perelman
11/ Sinclair Lewis

12/ Dashiell Hammett
13/ Franklin P. Adams
14/ Mark Twain
15/ Judge Crater
16/ Max Eastman
17/ Harold Ross
18/ James Thurber
19/ Edna St. Vincent Millay
20/ Max Eastman
21/ Thomas Wolfe
22/ Margaret Sanger

ber married **Helen Wismer**, and in the fall of that year they sublet a furnished $200-a-month apartment in a red brick building on this site. Here, Thurber mixed his steady writing for the *New Yorker* with continuous drinking and partying. By the summer of 1936, realizing New York was not good for them all the time, they moved to the Connecticut countryside. **Number 8** Fifth Avenue has been replaced by the modern apartments at 2 Fifth Avenue.

6/ Andre Kertesz
2 Fifth Ave. at West 8th Street.

Kertesz, one of the greatest photographers of this century, moved to the United States from his native Hungary in 1936 and lived on the 12th floor of this modern high-rise building from the early 1950's until his death in 1985. He was 91.

7/ Dashiell Hammett
24 Fifth Ave. at West 9th Street.

This apartment building used to be the **Fifth Avenue Hotel** and **Hammett** lived here in the early 1940's. During that period, he made a number of unsuccessful attempts to enlist in the army; he was finally accepted as a private in the fall of 1942 at the age of 48.

Hammett was sent to the Aleutian Islands where he became the editor of the camp newspaper.

8/ Marianne Moore, Anais Nin
35 W. 9th St. between Fifth and Sixth Avenue.

The poet **Marianne Moore** moved into this house in 1966 after living in Brooklyn for more than 35 years. She had left Brooklyn at the insistence of friends who felt that her neighborhood had become dangerous. She lived here on West 9th Street until her death in 1971 at age 84.

Writer **Anais Nin** also made this her home in the early 1950's.

9/ Elinor Wylie
36 W. 9th St. between Fifth and Sixth Avenue.

This house was the poet's last residence. She moved here with her husband, **William Rose Benet**, in 1926. She died here on December 16, 1928, at the age of 43.

10/ S.J. Perelman
64 W. 9th St. between Fifth and Sixth Avenue.

The humorist moved into an apartment here with his wife, **Laura West**, in 1929, just after their marriage. They stayed until 1930.

11/ Sinclair Lewis
37 W. 10th St. between Fifth and Sixth Avenue.

The man who wrote *Main Street* moved into this red brick rowhouse with his new wife, journalist **Dorothy Thompson**, in August, 1928. The large studio on the second floor became her work space.

Lewis rented a hotel room nearby as an office. They moved away in 1929.

12/ Dashiell Hammett
28 W. 10th St. between Fifth and Sixth Avenue.

Hammett moved into a duplex apartment in this four-story building in the fall of 1947. He was then teaching courses in mystery writing at the **Jefferson School of Social Science**. He was living here in 1951 when he was sent to prison for 22 weeks by a U.S. district court for refusing to answer questions about a leftist organization called the Civil Rights Congress of which he was a member. After serving his time, he returned to this apartment. He moved out in early 1952, unable to pay the rent.

13/ Franklin P. Adams
26 W. 10th St. between Fifth and Sixth Avenue.

Adams, one of America's most popular newspaper columnists and a prominent member of the **Algonquin Round Table**, lived in this brownstone house with his second wife and their four children from 1929 until the mid-1930's.

14/ Mark Twain
14 W. 10th St. between Fifth and Sixth Avenue.

Returning from a long trip to Europe with his wife in 1900, the author moved into this large red brick rowhouse. The house soon became one of the most conspicuous residences in New York because **Twain** was very famous by then.

There was a constant procession of callers, many of them strangers who came for an autograph or a handshake. Twain moved out of the house for good in the fall of 1901 because the upkeep was too strenuous for his wife. They moved to a house along the Hudson River outside the city.

15/ Judge Crater
40 Fifth Ave. at West 11th Street.

Judge Joseph F. Crater of the **New York State Supreme Court** lived in an apartment here in 1930 with his wife, **Stella**. On August 6 of that year he vanished, thus beginning one of the most controversial missing-person cases in U.S. history.

Stella temporarily became a suspect in her husband's possible murder but the case was never solved. It was officially closed in July, 1937, when he was declared legally dead. He was never found. For years after his disappearance, this building was a favorite tourist attraction. The entrance to the building is on 11th Street, across from the **First Presbyterian Church**.

16/ Max Eastman
27 W. 11th St. between Fifth and Sixth Avenue.

Eastman was only 29 in 1912 when he received this message from the artists and writers of the new journal, *The Masses:* "You are elected editor of The Masses. No pay."

Thus began the creation of one of the most famous American magazines. Eastman served as editor of the legendary literary and political journal for six years until 1917 when it was suppressed by the federal government during World War I. In the year that he became editor, he moved into a top-floor apartment here with his first wife, **Ida Rauh**. A baby son was born to them here.

It was in this apartment that Eastman first met and hired **John Reed** to write for *The Masses*. This building is across the street from the site at 18 W. 11th St. where on March 5, 1970, a bomb was set off accidentally by members of the radical underground group, the **"Weathermen."** The old house, built in 1845, was destroyed and three people were killed. A modern apartment building has replaced the old house.

17/ Harold Ross
56 W. 11th St. between Fifth and Sixth Avenue.

The first editor of the *New Yorker* lived in a small apartment in this building with his war-time friend **John Winterich** in 1919 after their discharge from the army. He worked first as an editor for a veterans' magazine and then in 1920 for the magazine of the **American Legion**. **Ross** moved away in the summer of 1920 when he married his first wife, **Jane Grant**. It wasn't until 1925 that they founded the *New Yorker*.

18/ James Thurber
65 W. 11th St. between Fifth and Sixth Avenue.

In 1928, not long after he was hired by **Harold Ross** to be the managing editor (and soon after, writer) for the *New Yorker*, **Thurber** and his first

wife, **Althea**, rented an apartment on this site where the **New School for Social Research** now stands. Because of growing tensions in their marriage, they moved away in 1929 to a house in Connecticut where she lived alone most of the time while Thurber stayed in New York hotels and visited her for short periods.

19/ Edna St. Vincent Millay
77 W. 12th St. at Sixth Avenue.

The poet moved to a "big lovely room" in a house on this site in September 1920. She had been living with her mother and two sisters near the Hudson River docks but she wanted to live alone so that there would be fewer things to distract her from her work. Soon after, her sister, **Kathleen,** moved in next door in the same building. **Millay** stayed here until January, 1921, when she sailed for Europe.

20/ Max Eastman
8 W. 13th St. near Fifth Avenue.

An apartment in this building was **Eastman's** home for the last 25 years of his life. Eastman was the editor of the literary and political journal, *The Masses,* from 1912 until 1917 (see Number 16 above). He died in 1969.

21/ Thomas Wolfe
27 W. 15th St. between Fifth and Sixth Avenue.

The novelist lived in a second floor room in this five-story white stone building just north of Greenwich Village from 1928 until 1930. It was here that he revised his manuscript of *Look Homeward, Angel* which was finally published in the fall of 1929. In 1930 he left for a long trip to Europe.

22/ Margaret Sanger
17 W. 16th St. near Fifth Avenue.

The pioneer in family planning and birth control opened her famous clinic in this old brownstone house just north of Greenwich Village in 1923.

Sanger converted the lower levels into offices and consulting rooms for her patients and made the top floor into an apartment. She maintained the clinic here until her death and, although she moved to other residences during her lifetime, she continued to use the apartment here over the years. Sanger died in Arizona in 1966 at age 86. **The Margaret Sanger Clinic** remained here until 1973.

Tour 4

1/ Franklin P. Adams
124 W. 13th St. between Sixth and Seventh Avenue.

The newspaper columnist lived on two floors of this red brick house with his second wife, **Esther**, from 1925 until 1928.

2/ E.B. White
112 W. 13th St. between Sixth and Seventh Avenue.

White moved into a third-floor apartment in this building with three fraternity brothers in 1925. He was a young unemployed writer at the time. One of **White's** idols was *New York World* columnist **Franklin P. Adams** who lived a few doors away at 124 W. 13th St. (see Number 1 above).

In those days, he wrote that New York hardly gave him a living, although he said, "it sustained me" and that for inspiration he used to walk quickly past Adams' house.

3/ S.J. Perelman
134 W. 11th St. between Sixth Avenue and Greenwich Avenue.

This brownstone building was the humorist's home from 1955 until 1966. It was here in 1955 that he wrote the screenplay of *Around the World in 80 Days.*

4/ Theodore Dreiser
118 W. 11th St. between Sixth Avenue and Greenwich Avenue.

Here, on the spot where the **Greenwich Village School** now stands, was a row of beautiful townhouses, called **Rhinelander Gardens**, built in 1854. **Dreiser** moved into a two-room apartment here in September, 1923. It was the place where he wrote most of his novel, *An American Tragedy.*

By 1927, its financial success allowed him to move to more expensive quarters uptown. Dreiser moved back here in 1937 for a short time, living in a dif-

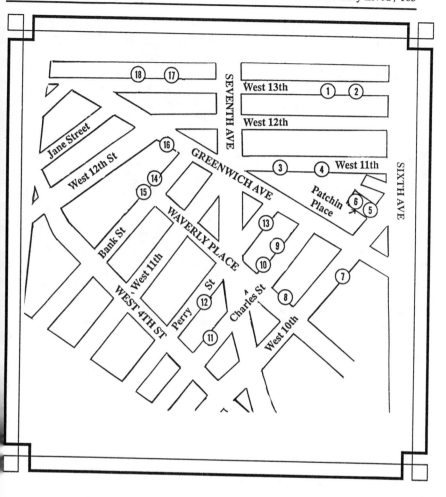

Tour 4

1/ Franklin P. Adams
2/ E.B. White
3/ S.J. Perelman
4/ Theodore Dreiser
5/ Reed and Bryant
6/ e.e. cummings
7/ Woody Guthrie
8/ Margaret Mead
9/ James Cain

10/ Richard Wright
11/ Fiorello LaGuardia
12/ James Agee
13/ Margaret Sanger
14/ Willa Cather
15/ John Dos Passos
16/ The Masses
17/ Anais Nin
18/ Edmund Wilson

ferent apartment. Rhinelander Gardens was torn down in 1955.

5/ John Reed and Louise Bryant
1 Patchin Place between Sixth Avenue and Greenwich Avenue off West 10th Street.

Patchin Place is a small enclosed courtyard just off West 10th Street containing 10 brick houses dating back to 1848.

After **Reed** returned from Russia in the spring of 1918, where he was reporting on the Russian Revolution, he took a small, dingy apartment here with **Bryant**. Reed was on trial at that time, along with *The Masses* editor **Max Eastman** and others, for conspiracy against the government. Two trials resulted in hung juries. Reed and Bryant spent much of their time on speaking tours promoting Bolshevism.

6/ e.e. cummings
4 Patchin Place between Sixth Avenue and Greenwich Avenue off West 10th Street.

After the poet returned from Europe in 1923, he moved into a studio on the top floor here. **Cummings** and his third wife, **Marion Morehouse**, eventually bought the entire house and he lived there for the rest of his life until his death in 1962.

Patchin Place has been the home of other writers, artists, and actors over the years.

Theodore Dreiser lived here for a short time. Avant-garde writer **Djuna Barnes** occupied a tiny room-and-a-

Reed

half apartment here from 1940 until her death in 1982 at the age of 90.

Marlon Brando shared an apartment here with his sister, **Frances**, in 1943 and 1944 while he studied drama at the New School for Social Research.

7/ Woody Guthrie
130 W. 10th St. near Greenwich Avenue.

This three-story red brick building, constructed in 1862, was the home of the folk singer in 1941-42. **Guthrie** lived here and performed with the legendary folk group, the **Almanac Singers**, led by **Pete Seeger**.

Called **Almanac House**, the place really functioned as a commune. Musicians, intellectuals, drunks, and all sorts of people down on their luck stopped here to enjoy the generous hospitality and sat in on the frequent hootenannies which took place in the basement.

8/ Margaret Mead
193 Waverly Place between West 10th and Charles Street.

America's most renowned anthropologist rented a floor in this attractive four-story brick house from 1955 until 1966. She lived here as a single parent with her 16-year-old daughter, **Cathy**, and another family. In 1966 **Mead** moved away from Greenwich Village to 211 Central Park West where she lived for the rest of her life (see Section Four, Tour 2, Number 9).

9/ James Cain
11 Charles St. between Greenwich Avenue and Waverly Place.

The novelist who wrote *The Postman Only Rings Twice* and *Double Indemnity* lived in a three-room apartment on this block (called Van Nest Place then) from 1925 until 1927.

Cain, then working as a journalist for the *New York World* had just separated from his first wife, **Mary Clough**, and had fallen in love with a young Finnish emigre named **Elina Sjosted Tyszecka** who spoke little English. Cain and Elina would meet at the apartment here, happy to be together even though they were unable to talk to each other.

In 1927, Cain divorced his wife and married Elina. They moved to an apartment uptown.

10/ Richard Wright
13 Charles St. at Waverly Place.

The black novelist who wrote *Native Son* successfully bucked the odds of racial prejudice in this neighborhood and managed to obtain a mortgage and purchase a brownstone house on this site in 1947. He moved in with his wife, **Ellen**, and their young daughter, **Julia**, for a brief period, but soon decided to sell it and move to France, which became his home for the rest of his life.

In 1960, he died in Paris of a heart attack at the age of 52. His house has been replaced by this modern apartment building numbered 15 Charles Street.

11/ Fiorello LaGuardia
39 Charles St. between Seventh Avenue and West Fourth Street.

New York's colorful mayor from 1934 to 1945 lived in a four-room apartment here from 1914 until 1921.

He was a young private attorney and a bachelor when he moved in. In 1916 he was elected U.S. Congressman representing this district and in 1919 he became president of the New York City Board of Aldermen. Earlier that year, he married his first wife, **Thea Almerigotta**, and she moved into the apartment with him.

Here they entertained a small circle of friends, including **Enrico Caruso**, a regular visitor. By the end of 1920 both his wife and young child had developed tuberculosis and, for the sake of their health, the **LaGuardias** moved to a house in a rural section of the Bronx. Both wife and child died in 1921.

12/ James Agee
38 Perry St. between West 4th Street and Waverly Place (Seventh Avenue.)

Late in 1932, **Agee**, just out of Harvard and beginning a new job as writer for *Fortune* magazine, moved into a basement apartment in this four-story brick building. He married his first wife, **Via**, in January, 1933, and she moved here with him.

Their home consisted of two large, dark rooms, a kitchen, and a shaded back porch. In 1936, while living here, Agee traveled south with photographer **Walker Evans** to write the accounts of tenant farmers that later became the book, *Let Us Now Praise Famous Men*. Agee and Via separated late in 1937 and both moved away at the same time.

13/ Margaret Sanger
4 Perry St. near Greenwich Avenue.

The birth control pioneer was 34 when she rented an apartment in this brick building in 1914. It was during this period that she began to publish the feminist newspaper, *The Woman Rebel.*

14/ Willa Cather
5 Bank St. at Waverly Place.

From 1913 until 1927, the novelist lived in a spacious seven-room apartment on the second floor of a five-story brick house on this site. She shared it with her lifelong companion, **Edith Lewis**

It was during this period here that she wrote many of her most important books including *O Pioneers!*, *My An*

Cather

tonia, and *A Lost Lady*. **Cather** and Lewis moved away in 1927 when their building was torn down for this high-rise apartment building (numbered 1-7) that went up in 1928.

15/ John Dos Passos
11 Bank St. between Waverly Place and West Fourth Street.

The young author lived in this four-story brick apartment building for a few months starting in the fall of 1924. He had just returned from France and was almost broke. He worked on his novel *Manhattan Transfer* while he lived here. Early in 1925, he moved to Brooklyn.

16/ The Masses office
91 Greenwich Ave. between Bank Street and West 12th Street.

The famous radical magazine of arts and politics was published in a building on this site from 1912 until 1916. *The Masses,* which had about 20,000 subscribers at the height of its popularity, was probably the most important voice of bohemian and left-wing ideas in the early years of the century. Its editor, **Max Eastman**, lived just three blocks away at 27 W. 11th St. *The Masses* published its last issue in December, 1917. It was suppressed by the U.S. government because of its opposition to America's entry into World War I.

17/ Anais Nin
215 W. 13th St. between Seventh Avenue and Greenwich Avenue.

Shortly after returning from France in 1940, **Nin** rented a studio apartment on the top floor of this six-story build-ing covered with climbing plants. She described it as a "sort of walk-up studio penthouse with roof terrace." It was skylighted and rented for $60 a month. Nin lived here until 1948 when she moved temporarily to California. It was during her years here that she set up her own printing press and began publishing her writings. (See this section, Tour 1, No. 1.)

18/ Edmund Wilson
229 W. 13th St. between Seventh Avenue and Greenwich Avenue (and 224 W. 13th St.).

The critic moved into a room in this four-story building in 1925 after separating from his first wife, actress **Mary Blair. Wilson** was writing for the *New Republic* whose offices were only a couple of blocks away. (No. 229 has been renumbered; the **Integral Yoga Institute** is housed in this building now.) In 1929, Wilson moved across the street to a cheap furnished room at 224 W. 13th St

Tour 5

1/ Clifford Odets
82 Horatio St. between Washington and Greenwich Street.

The playwright was 27 in 1933 when he rented a tiny, airless apartment in this building next to a stable. (The stable is gone.)

It was his first apartment in New York, and he paid for the first month with option money received for his first play, *Awake and Sing!* **Odets** was then an actor and writer in the **Group Theater**.

He was still living here when he wrote *Waiting for Lefty* in 1934. Odets moved to a larger, more expensive apartment just before the Group Theater produced these two plays for the first time in 1935.

2/ John Cheever
633 Hudson St. at Jane Street.

In 1930, at the age of 18, **Cheever** arrived in New York City determined to be a writer. He rented a room in an old building on this site for $3 a week.

Tour 5

1/ Clifford Odets
2/ John Cheever
3/ Diane Arbus
4/ Carson McCullers
5/ Lee Strasberg
6/ Thomas Wolfe
7/ Margaret Mead

8/ Sinclair Lewis
9/ Woody Guthrie
10/ Delmore Schwartz
11/ Diane Arbus
12/ Bret Harte
13/ Hart Crane

When he couldn't afford the rent, he moved out and stayed with friends. According to his daughter, every day "he bought a bottle of milk and marked it into five portions to make it last."

Malcolm Cowley, then an editor for *The New Republic*, published Cheever's first short story in October, 1930. Number 633 Hudson is gone--replaced by this newer building numbered 61 Jane St.

3/ Diane Arbus
463 West St. between Bank and Bethune Street.

Westbeth is a huge, 13-story industrial building overlooking the Hudson River docks that was converted into an artists' community housing complex in 1965.

Arbus moved into a large duplex here on the ninth floor facing the river in January, 1970. It was the photographer's last home; she committed suicide here on July 26, 1971. She was only 48.

4/ Carson McCullers
321 W. 11th St. between Washington Street and Greenwich Street.

The Southern novelist lived on the top floor of this building in 1940 with her husband, **Roger**. It was the year that her first novel, *The Heart is a Lonely Hunter*, was published. This house dates back to 1838.

5/ Lee Strasberg and Clifford Odets
285 W. 11th St. at Bleecker Street.

In 1932, **Strasberg**, then director of the **Group Theater**, and his second wife, actress **Paula Miller**, moved into a small apartment above **Suttor's Bakery** in this four-story brick building.

Odets was then a young actor with the same theater and, needing a place to stay, moved in with them. Odets was the first of a long list of gifted artists--- to include **John Garfield, James Baldwin, Shelly Winters, Kim Stanley, Geraldine Page**, and **Marilyn Monroe**---for whom the Strasbergs would provide shelter over the years.

6/ Thomas Wolfe
263 W. 11th St. between Bleecker and West Fourth Street.

In October 1927, **Wolfe**, then teaching at **New York University** and struggling to complete his novel, *Look Homeward, Angel*, moved into a comfortable, second-floor apartment here with his companion, **Aline Bernstein**.

She used the front room as her studio, while Wolfe occupied the rear room overlooking a garden. By pushing himself to exhaustion, Wolfe finished his book in March, 1928. He moved away from here in June 1928 and traveled in Europe for the rest of that year.

7/ Margaret Mead
72 Perry St. between Bleecker and West Fourth Street.

The famous anthropologist moved into this four-story white brick house with her third husband, anthropologist **Gregory Bateson**, and their children in 1939. They lived here in a communal setting with another large family. **Mead** and Bateson were divorced in 1950 but Mead continued to live here until 1955.

8/ Sinclair Lewis
69 Charles St. between Bleecker and West Fourth Street.

Lewis came to New York as a young writer in 1910 and rented a small room in this gray-brick building. (The block was known as **Van Nest Place** then.)

His job as a manuscript reader for a commercial publisher paid $12.50 a week. Lewis lived here until 1913.

Fame didn't come until 1920 when *Main Street* was published.

9/ Woody Guthrie
74 Charles St. between Bleecker and West Fourth Street.

The singer and songwriter rented a small apartment---a fourth-floor walkup---here in 1943. It went for $27 per month.

About this time, **Guthrie** formed a new singing group made up of **Sonny Terry**, **Brownie McGhee**, and **Leadbelly**.

The new group didn't perform much in those days but instead sat around Woody's apartment drinking rye whiskey, eating beans and ham hocks, and singing through many long nights.

Guthrie's book, *Bound for Glory*, was published during his stay here.

Lewis

10/ Delmore Schwartz
75 Charles St. between Bleecker and West Fourth Street.

The poet lived in a book-lined apartment with high ceilings in this building from 1948 until 1951. It was during this period that he married his second wife, **Elizabeth**. He taught at the **New School for Social Research**.

11/ Diane Arbus
121 1/2 Charles St. at Greenwich Street.

After her separation from her husband, **Allan**, the photographer moved with her two daughters into a small reconverted stable here in the summer of 1959. She gave the girls the upstairs bedrooms; she slept in the living room. They lived here for the next 10 years, moving out in June, 1968.

12/ Bret Harte
487 Hudson St. at Grove Street.

Harte, journalist and author of such stories of the California Gold Rush as *The Luck of Roaring Camp* and *The Outcasts of Poker Flat,* lived in this now-restored Federal-style house during the 1870's. It stands next to the **Church of St. Luke-in-the-Fields**.

13/ Hart Crane
45 Grove St. at Bleecker Street.

Moving to New York from Cleveland, the poet rented a room from his friend, **Gorham Munson**, in this historic 150-year-old, five-story mansion, in early 1923.

It was here that he began writing his poem, *The Bridge.* Mostly without funds for three months, **Crane** finally obtained a clerical position in a large advertising agency and soon moved away to larger quarters.

Tour 6

1/ Edna St. Vincent Millay
75 1/2 Bedford St. at Commerce Street.

This building, erected in 1873 and only 9 1/2-feet wide, is thought to be the narrowest house in the city.

It is also identified with **Millay** who moved here in November, 1923, with her husband, **Eugen Boissevain**, soon after their marriage. It was her last New York City residence; in June 1925 the poet and her husband moved to a country house in Austerlitz, New York where she remained for the rest of her life.

The house next door, on the corner, (77 Bedford Street) was built in 1800 and is the oldest house in Greenwich Village.

Millay
Just 9 1/2 feet at 75 1/2 Bedford St.

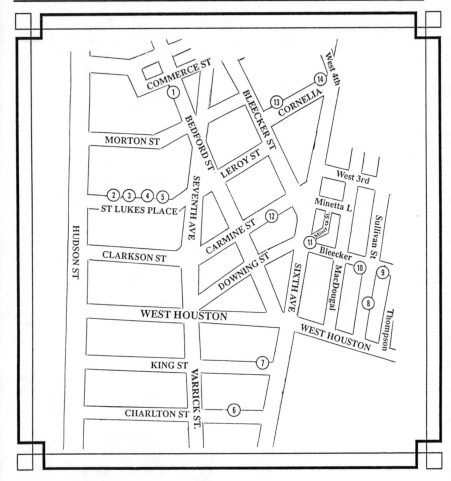

Tour 6

1/ **Edna St. Vincent Millay**
2/ **Jimmy Walker**
3/ **Sherwood Anderson**
4/ **Marianne Moore**
5/ **Theodore Dreiser**
6/ **Edna St. Vincent Millay**
7/ **James Agee**

8/ **Fiorello LaGuardia**
9/ **Theodore Dreiser**
10/ **James Agee**
11/ **Reader's Digest**
12/ **Jackson Pollock**
13/ **James Agee**
14/ **W.H. Auden**

2/ Jimmy Walker

6 St. Luke's Place between Hudson Street and Seventh Avenue.

St. Luke's Place is one of New York's most pleasant streets with its charming group of 15 Italianate row houses that date back to the early 1850's.

Walker, New York's colorful Democratic mayor from 1926 until 1932 was born here and made it his home until 1932 when, under a cloud of scandal, he was forced to resign. He then fled to Europe to live with his second wife, former showgirl **Betty Compton**.

The house remained in the family until 1934.

3/ Sherwood Anderson

12 St. Luke's Place between Hudson Street and Seventh Avenue.

In the summer of 1923, the author lived in a basement apartment here.

He had already seen his novel, *Winesburg, Ohio*, published but little or no money had come in. He continued to hold his job in a Chicago advertising agency and after saving a little money would "run away" for a time.

He was offered the use of this apartment at a very cheap rent when its occupants, two young professors at Columbia, went away for the summer.

One of his neighbors that year was fellow author, **Theodore Dreiser**, who lived a few doors away at No. 16 (See Number 5 below).

4/ Marianne Moore

14 St. Luke's Place between Hudson Street and Seventh Avenue.

The poet lived here with her mother in a ground-floor apartment from 1918 until 1929.

While writing poetry, she worked as a secretary in a private girls' school and as a tutor. Then from 1921 to 1925 she worked half-days at the Hudson Park branch of the *New York Public Library* opposite her apartment. In 1925, she became editor of the literary magazine, the *Dial*. **Moore** and her mother moved to Brooklyn in 1929 where she lived until 1966.

5/ Theodore Dreiser

16 St. Luke's Place between Hudson Street and Seventh Avenue.

The novelist took a two-room apartment in this building in October, 1922, and stayed until late 1923. It was here that he began to write *An American Tragedy*.

The place was the scene of one of the most unusual parties of the 1920's. Present were such notable writers as **H.L. Mencken, Sherwood Anderson, and F. Scott Fitzgerald**. Although there are conflicting accounts of the event, all agreed that **Dreiser** provided no refreshments, introduced no one to anyone, and remained completely silent while his guests, seated along the wall, waited for something to happen. Fitzgerald arrived with champagne, which Dreiser promptly put in his icebox. After another endless wait, everyone left---one-by-one.

6/ Edna St. Vincent Millay
25 Charlton St. between Varrick Street and Sixth Avenue.

From June, 1918, until January, 1919, the poet lived on the top floor of this three-story red brick house with her mother, **Cora**, and two sisters, **Norma** and **Kathleen**.

During this period she was busy acting, writing, and directing for the **Provincetown Players**.

7/ James Agee
17 King St. at Sixth Avenue.

In September, 1953, the writer purchased this old house and moved in with his third wife, **Mia Fritsch**, and his two young daughters.

The house had been built by **Aaron Burr**, who is reputed to have hidden in it after killing **Alexander Hamilton** in a duel.

Agee, then in poor health from alcohol and a recent heart attack, was working as a screenwriter. He was living here when, on May 16, 1955, he suffered a heart attack in a taxicab. He died in the hospital soon after. He was 45.

8/ Fiorello LaGuardia
177 Sullivan St. between Bleecker Street and West Houston Street.

New York's greatest mayor was born on this site on December 11, 1882. He was the son of a Jewish mother and an Italian father. His parents had come to the U.S. from Italy two years earlier.

LaGuardia

LaGuardia only lived in this tenement flat for three years as a child because his father, a musician, was unable to find work and finally in 1885 joined the U.S. Army as chief bandmaster of the **Eleventh Infantry Regiment**.

The family moved west to Dakota Territory and Fiorello didn't see New York again for 21 years. The old building here collapsed in 1988 during renovation.

9/ Theodore Dreiser
160 Bleecker St. between Sullivan and Thompson Street.

This luxury apartment house called the **Atrium** was built in 1892 as the **Mills House**, where poor transients could get a bed for the night in one of its 1500 rooms for twenty-five cents.

Dreiser was a down-and-out 24-year-old writer in 1895 when he stayed here on his first visit to New York. He soon landed a job as a magazine editor. Dreiser returned here to live briefly in 1903 during another difficult period of his life. Later, Mills House became the **Greenwich Hotel**.

The famous **Village Gate** cabaret opened here in the basement during the late 1950's. The cabaret featured folk, jazz, and blues music, and nurtured some of America's most famous comedians during their early careers including **Woody Allen, Bill Cosby, Dick Gregory**, and **Richard Prior**.

10/ James Agee
172 Bleecker St. at Sullivan Street.

In the fall of 1941, soon after his second wife, **Alma,** moved away from him, Agee took a fifth floor apartment in this red brick building with his new lover, **Mia Fritsch** , who was later to be his third wife.

At the time they moved in, his book, *Let Us Now Praise Famous Men*, done in collaboration with photographer **Walker Evans**, was published. Agee soon became the movie critic for both *Time Magazine* and *The Nation*.

By the late 1940's, he gave up these jobs to write for the movies. In 1951 he wrote the screenplay for **John Huston's** *The African Queen*. Agee kept his apartment here until 1951.

11/ Reader's Digest
1 Minetta St. at Sixth Avenue.

In 1922, in a basement apartment located under a speakeasy here, **DeWitt Wallace** and his wife, **Lila Acheson**, with money borrowed from relatives, set up editorial offices and proceeded to produce the first issue of a magazine called the *Reader's Digest*.

When the first 5,000 copies arrived from the printer, Wallace hired bar girls from the speakeasy to help him and Lila wrap and address them. The response to the new publication was immediate and, within a short time, the Wallaces were managing one of the most popular magazines in publishing history.

12/ Jackson Pollock
46 Carmine St. between Bleecker Street and Bedford Street.

The abstract expressionist painter lived in an apartment in this three-story building in 1932 and 1933 as a young man. The neighborhood was mainly Italian in those days. **Pollock** was studying at the **Art Students League** at that time.

13/ James Agee
33 Cornelia St. between Bleecker and West Fourth Street.

During the mid-1940's, while **Agee** lived on Bleecker Street (see No. 10 above), he rented a studio in this house.

It was here that he did most of his writing. It was furnished with a gas stove and fireplace. Agee continued to use it in the early 1950's.

14/ W.H. Auden
7 Cornelia St. near West Fourth Street.

The poet moved into a small apartment on the fourth floor of this building in 1946. It consisted of a bedsitting room and a small kitchen and when **Tennessee Williams** visited **Auden**, he described it as "fantastically sordid...with beer cans and newspapers all about the floor." Auden's book, *The Age of Anxiety*, was published during his residence here. He moved away in 1953.

Tour 7

((The East Village)

The **East Village** is adjacent to Greenwich Village, east of the **Bowery** and **Third Avenue**, between **Houston Street** and **East 14th Street**.

1/ George and Ira Gershwin

91 Second Ave. between 5th and 6th Street.

This red brick building with the store front on the ground level is one of the early homes of the **Gershwin** family. In 1910, when **George** was age 12 and **Ira** was 14, they were living on the second story here above a phonograph shop.

One day a van appeared, unloaded a piano and hoisted it up to the Gershwin apartment. It had been purchased by Mrs. Gershwin.

"No sooner had it come through the window and been backed up against the wall than I was at the keys," George recalled. "I must have crowded out Ira very soon for the plan originally had been to start him off on the instrument."

George learned to play it almost immediately without the benefit of lessons. Only six years later, he published his first song.

2/ Mark Rothko

313 E. 6th St. between First and Second Avenue.

The abstract expressionist painter lived in this four-story red brick building with his first wife, **Edith Sachar**, from 1936 to 1940.

She was a designer of costume jewelry; this residence functioned as his studio and her shop. He was still virtually an unknown painter at the time.

3/ W.H. Auden

77 St. Mark's Place near First Avenue.

The poet was 46 when he moved into a four-room apartment on the second floor here in 1953.

It was in the basement of this same

Auden at 77 St. Mark's Place
In the basement, Trostsky

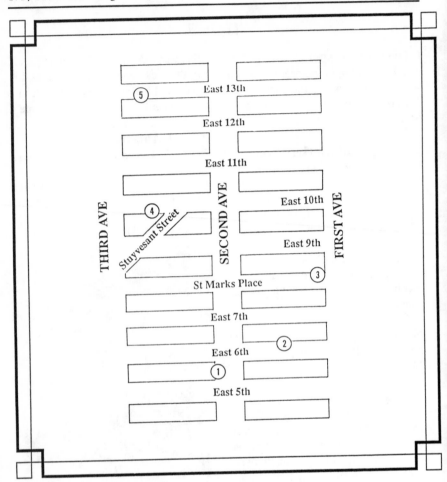

Tour 7

1/ George Gershwin   4/ Diane Arbus
2/ Mark Rothko   5/ Emma Goldman
3/ W.H. Auden

building in 1917 that Russian revolutionist, **Leon Trotsky**, printed the newspaper, *Novy Mir*. A few months later he returned to Russia to participate in the **Bolshevik Revolution**.

Auden said that he liked his apartment here more than anywhere else he had lived in New York. He was a parishioner at the beautiful church, **St. Mark's-in-the-Bouwerie**, located a few blocks away at Second Avenue and East 11th Street.

Auden lived here at 77 St. Mark's Place until April, 1972, when he left the U.S. permanently to live in Great Britain. He died in September 1973.

4/ Diane Arbus
120 E. 10th St. between Second and Third Avenue.

The photographer was 45 in 1968 when she moved to a duplex apartment on the top floor of this building. She lived here until 1970. **Arbus** died in 1971 (see this section, Tour 5, Number 3).

5/ Emma Goldman
210 E. 13th St. near Third Avenue.

The famed anarchist and feminist lived in an apartment on the sixth floor of this old building (now numbered 208) from 1903 until 1913.

She published her journal, *Mother Earth*, here starting in 1906. In that same year, her anarchist colleague and lover, **Alexander Berkman**, was released from prison and joined her here. Berkman had served 14 years for the attempted assassination of industrialist **Henry Clay Frick** in 1892.

Goldman's apartment was known as the "home for lost dogs" because many people who had little money and no place to stay often ended up here. It became a gathering place for Greenwich Village radicals and intellectuals.

Goldman

Acknowledgments

Many people supported me in the writing of this book. Unfortunately I cannot name them all in this limited space. Therefore, I will confine my thanks to those individuals who had a direct hand in the final result.

My expression of gratitude must begin with an acknowledgment to the person who made the appearance of this book possible. Marlin Bree not only took the risk of publishing it but also patiently and expertly guided me on the difficult steps along the way.

The following people provided important assistance to me in a number of specific areas: Ruth Caprow, whose drawings have, I feel, added a lyrical touch to this endeavor; Chuck Hovland, a New York City resident, who researched a number of addresses when I was unable to do so myself; Gregg Shadduck, John Wickre, and John Fierst, who supplied me with invaluable computer expertise; Gary Swanson, who helped me with the maps; and Ed Denn, who gave me excellent legal advice.

Nell Abell, Mary Kay Elling, and the family of John Goggin, Julie Weighter, and their daughter Alycia, not only offered me good counsel all along the way but, more importantly, kept me laughing.

Thanks to both my entire family and the staff of the James Jerome Hill Reference Library for their kind and solid support of me during the writing of this book. In particular, thanks to Paul Wittkopf, head of public services at the library, for giving me the flexible work schedule that I needed to research it.

I want to acknowledge my special indebtedness to the following people: Ardis Jensen, who aided in the editing of the original text; Lucille Swanson, my sister, who typed many pages of text in the early stages; and Myrna Liebers, whose sense of discovery inspired me as we walked some of the streets of Manhattan. All three, in addition, offered endless good cheer.

Finally, my deepest gratitude is reserved for two people. Carol Morgan helped me develop the original idea for this project and gave me sound and practical advice, editorial and otherwise, all along the way. Wendy Adamson not only provided me with technical and editorial assistance but offered constant encouragement and enthusiasm. Without Carol's support, I would never have started this book. Without Wendy's support, I would never have completed it.

Stephen W. Plumb
Author

INDEX OF PLACES

INDEX OF PERSONS

Notes

Notes

About the Author: Stephen W. Plumb is a reference librarian at the James Jerome Hill Reference Library in St. Paul, Minnesota. He is a former director of the State of Minnesota's Legislative Reference Library and was also a newspaper librarian at the *Minneapolis Star-Trib*.

This book came about because of Mr. Plumb's longstanding interest in Manhattan. In exploring the city during a visit, he realized the need for identifying the homes and haunts of the many legendary individuals he had encountered in his readings---people who had lived and worked in the very neighborhoods through which he walked.

From this beginning, the author researched scores of authoritative biographies, autobiographies, biographical directories, as well as other reference sources, to find information about the places associated with more than 400 famous New Yorkers. This effort was followed by numerous trips to Manhattan to verify the addresses and the current status of the 500 residences chartered in the book. Mr. Plumb is an inveterate walker.